T0285308

DARE TO
BECOME

DARE TO
BECOME

JULIE CROPP GARELECK

THE
ST●RY
PLANT
ATLANTA, GEORGIA

Story Plant hardcover ISBN-13: 978-1-61188-401-2
Story Plant e-book ISBN-13: 978-1-61188-418-0

The Library of Congress Cataloguing-in-Publication Data
is available upon request.

First Story Plant Printing: September 2024
Printed in the United States of America
0 9 8 7 6 5 4 3 2 1

1270 Caroline Street
Suite D120-381
Atlanta, GA 30307

Visit our website at www.TheStoryPlant.com

This book is dedicated to those who aspire to be—
and dare to become.

TABLE OF CONTENTS

CHAPTER ONE

AN INTRODUCTION

Success isn't a destination. It's a journey that often starts with a simple moment. A moment that has the potential to forever shape the trajectory of your life.

It was 1995. As a 16-year-old, growing up in the small town of Gettysburg, Pennsylvania –a town with less than 7,500 residents—it was customary to attend church on Sundays, walk around at high school football games on Friday night, and find a summer job to serve the one million tourists who visited our historic township each year. It was the only way to keep idle hands and minds occupied and to stave off the onslaught of insufferable teenage angst and boredom.

I was the youngest child in our middle-class family, with two working parents and my sister, now finishing her freshman year of college. My father was the general manager of a growing division of a Fortune 1000 company and my mother a bank teller. I was finishing up my junior year of high school. An idyllic and innocent time to soak up my childhood and to celebrate my rising senior year in high school status.

It was an average day. Before dinner, my parents called my sister and me into their bedroom. We immediately sensed that something was wrong. We never went into my parents' bedroom unless we were sick or about to get in serious trouble. My sister and I sat on the cedar chest at the foot of the bed, as they sat perched on each side of the bed in front of us. I remember looking at my sister to see if she had any idea what this family meeting was about.

After a few minutes of awkward silence, my dad said, "Well, girls. Do you want the good news or the bad news?" My sister and I looked at each other and shrugged. One of us uttered to give us the bad news. Dad proceeded to say, "I've quit my job."

I'm certain we gasped even though the silence was deafening in that moment. The good news, he went on to say, was that he decided to make an investment that included buying the Avenue Restaurant, a local 110-seat family restaurant, originally a diner from the 1950s. Curiously, it was a restaurant that he had never eaten in, yet it was the place where my best friend and I went for cheesecake before cheering at a football or basketball game.

As my parents continued to explain what the new plan was going to be, my mind was racing. Was Dad having a midlife crisis in his 40s? Could he afford my sister's college tuition? How about me? Would I be able to go to college? What did all of this mean? Is this his opportunity to leave an incredibly stressful and thankless job that took him on the road 40% of the time, away from our home? Over the last 10 years, in addition to my dad's full-time job, my parents had bought and sold residential homes, fixed them up, and sold them to earn extra income. But now, buying a restaurant seemed like a bit of a reach.

As I turned my focus back to the conversation, my dad asked my sister and me, "Are you in?" Blank stares. "This is only going to work if we are all in this together." Without hesitation, we both replied "YES!"

I can assure you that, at the time, I was completely unaware of the significance of this conversation and totally unprepared for the life lessons I was about to learn.

The Avenue Restaurant was a local staple, located on Steinwehr Avenue, once considered the historic pathway in Gettysburg, and which was prime real estate at the time. The Avenue, as we called it, had been around since 1956 with only two previous owners. We served breakfast, lunch, and dinner. The doors opened at 6am and closed at 8pm, seven days a week. Like most of the property investments my parents had made, the Avenue received quite the overhaul from the kitchen systems to the dining room décor.

Resistant to change, I continued to work at the local Gettysburg Tour Center for June of that summer in protest. That is, of course, until I worked a weekend shift to help my parents out and realized just how much money waitresses could make on a busy Sunday morning. Excitedly, I told my parents I wanted to come to work at the Avenue, hoping to secure a morning shift. But to my chagrin, the Avenue already had a stable of waitresses who had worked the same shifts for over 20 years. I was relegated to restaurant hostess to watch and learn from the veteran team. A veteran team that was far less interested in working with a 16-year-old, glass-half-full, high school cheerleader and boss's daughter.

I showed up to work with a smile on my face and gracefully tiptoed around the people politics. When an employee didn't show up, it fell upon me to serve as dishwasher on mornings where the temperature gauge read 120 degrees in the kitchen. I peeled 50 pounds of boiled potatoes until I had calluses on my hands. I buttered toast for the waitresses, filled drink orders, sorted silverware, refilled containers, cleaned counters, bused tables, and mopped the greasy floors in between shifts. I was quite possibly in hell.

When I wasn't working, I was sleeping or trying to salvage any high school social plans I could feasibly squeeze into the very limited open time I had. I cried on some occasions, jealous of my high school friends who were on vacation, lying in the sun, and drinking in the summer before our senior year.

At some point, midway through my senior year, I finally managed to get two evening waitressing shifts a week. I'd go to school, finish team practice, work a four-hour shift, and head home to tackle any homework I wasn't able to get done at school. I even managed to work in a social life on the weekends from 9pm to 11pm. My discontent for the perceived unfairness began to settle in as I accepted this unasked-for role in the family business. Within 18 months, the restaurant had grown significantly to serve between 98,000 and 112,000 meals each year. The days were grueling, long, and at times impossible. I remember many nights being too tired to eat the food we'd served all day; my parents, sister, and I would walk up the street to the local, family-run pizza place. We'd commiserate over the day, discuss how to improve our processes, and share an interesting conversation we'd had with a customer. As a family, we were together, but we were always working or, even worse, just thinking and talking about work.

But then something funny happened. As I finally began to embrace my role, I began to thrive in this environment. I listened and learned from the employees and my customers. I developed friendships with our regulars and with travelers who visited Gettysburg several times a year. Being something of a natural-born people person, I met and spoke with so many people from all different walks of life. I easily navigated personalities and internal politics. I managed through difficult situations, even dealing with perpetual sexual harassment from the so-called "trusted" employees who we employed. I grew a thicker skin and a stronger voice. Why? Because, in a sense, I had to.

For the duration of my college career, at Shippensburg University, I worked at the restaurant, finally securing the coveted Sunday morning shift I had waited years to get. Afraid of losing my slot, I would wake up at 5 am on Sunday morning, almost always after having gone to bed at 3am, and drive the 40 minutes home to work my shift. I would run to my parents' house at 2pm for a shower and a quick nap, while I did my laundry. Wake up at 5pm to drive back to campus for a sorority meeting.

As you might imagine, this schedule was not easy to maintain. The constant and ongoing pressure that came with this family business often conflicted with the idyllic concept of being a carefree college student. The truth is, I cried most of the Sunday evening drives back to school, feeling completely overwhelmed. By the time I finally reached the edge of campus, I'd pull myself together and remind myself that my life had fared better than most. I adopted the phrase "I'm fine, it's fine, it's all going to be fine." If I repeated it enough times, it would be enough for me to reset and start again.

I vividly remember the Christmas of my junior year. My friends were all planning New Year's parties over the break. Immediately disappointed and jealous, I knew I would be working through the entire break. It was the one time each year that the restaurant closed to perform maintenance, renovations, etc. I was disagreeable to say the least. Instead of sleeping in during the vacation, I had to be up and at work before 8am for what I knew would be a 10-hour shift. I huffed and puffed like a pouting child. My mom handed me a bucket of bleach water and a toothbrush, pointing to the tile floor. I looked at her incredulously.

Since we had reupholstered the booths, the grout on the tile floor now looked dingy and dirty. My task was to scrub two-by-two tile grout lines, the span of the 2,000-square-foot floor, with a toothbrush until they were gleaming white. Tears burned my eyes as I took on the chore, likely from both the deep personal frustration I felt as well as from the intense and pungent smell of the bleach water. I mumbled expletives under my breath as I went scrubbing on my knees, tile by tile.

But as the hours went on, I actually started to see the fruits of my labor. Those grout lines looked like new. The floors were once again restored to their original splendor. After we reopened, customers would even comment on how clean the floors were. I'd be lying if it didn't make me smile a bit and feel pride for a hard day's work.

⌐

Much like four years before when I was in high school, I was now focused on the spring before my senior year in college. My sorority was planning a big trip to Cancun, Mexico, for spring break. Other sororities and fraternities would also be headed to the same area. It was going to be a vacation of epic proportions. It was going to be full of memories of a lifetime! But I also knew it was a trip I would never ask to go on because I was already scheduled to work at the restaurant.

While my entire social network was enjoying all that spring break entails, I was back home, working at the Avenue. I did, however, save enough money from my labors to finally buy a brand-new car. My parents would cosign, but I was responsible for the down payment, monthly payments, and insurance. It was truly the silver lining that I needed. I was subjected to the retelling of that spring break trip for the rest of my college experience. Each time I heard the stories, I felt even more disconnected and much like an outsider. *"I'm fine, it's fine, it's all going to be fine."*

⌐

As I neared the end of college, I had dreams of leaving this small college town behind to explore all that this great world had to offer. I had declared a major in journalism, committed to my life's dream of becoming a reporter, and I had minored in French as an homage to my passion for all things French. As friends started interviewing and securing jobs after college, I didn't know what my next move was. When asked, I would tell people that I'd love to escape to Paris and find a job in my field. "No, seriously. What are you going to do?" My boyfriend at the time scoffed that my earning potential would only ever be $35,000/year as a communications major. Was I imaginative? Yes. Did I have high expectations for what life had to offer me? Yes. Was I afraid of heading from one small town back to my hometown? Yes. The stress and pressure were becoming intolerable.

I walked out of a language class, scanning the bulletin boards on the way out of the building. I noticed a poster from Boston University promoting a rigorous eight-week language intensive course with the opportunity to be placed in a job in your field. I grabbed one of the cards and immediately scheduled a meeting with my advisor. I told her I was interested in pursuing this opportunity and inquired about what was needed to get my application in. She pushed back from her chair and placed her hands neatly on her lap. She said, "Julie, you aren't an honor student and, quite frankly, as an average student from a state school, you have little chance of being accepted."

Thankful for my thick skin and stronger voice, I ignored her counsel. I just pushed on and asked her for the application.

As part of the application, I was asked to provide an essay on why I wanted to attend this program at Boston University. I poured my soul into this essay, written completely in French. The words I wrote spoke to my dreams and what I'd hope to gain with this once-in-a-lifetime experience.

After submitting the application paperwork, the waiting game began. It was excruciating, waiting, and hoping every day for any kind of word to arrive. I'm sure my friends—like the college career counselor—probably thought I was delusional. But then one day, everything in my life changed! My dad and sister (now home working the family business) called me one afternoon to tell me that I had been accepted into the program. A letter had arrived at our home with the details of what was to come.

I would later learn that more than 1,100 students applied and only 18 were accepted. I was one of two students from state schools and the first from my school to be accepted into this program.

In that summer of 2000, the year I graduated from college, I worked 80 hours a week at the Avenue. By now, the word had spread of my acceptance into the French program; my regular customers and seasonal customers were so excited for me and my upcoming adventure. Many of my customers had become friends. We shared many stories over the years. They watched me grow from high school right through college. What used to be merely dreams for me had now become a reality.

I was finally—*finally!*—on my way. And to France of all places!

It was as though I was going from one end of the world's spectrum, that of working endless hours at the Avenue Restaurant in small-town Gettysburg, Pennsylvania, to the total opposite end of the globe, that of living and working under the glitzy lights and high glamour of Paris!

It's funny. Looking back now, as a successful entrepreneur, little did I ever realize that as much as I couldn't wait to escape the long, long hours and hard work at the family restaurant, those experiences at the Avenue would actually result in having been a great and meaningful training ground for me as I embarked on my career. It was as though those long and difficult years had evolved into my own "home schooled" version of an MBA program.

CHAPTER TWO

⌒

OFF TO THE BIG CITY!

By August, I packed up my two oversized suitcases and embarked on my journey to France. Acclimating to the fast-paced hustle of Paris was easier than I thought it would be, although adapting to speaking only French was much harder than I had imagined, despite having successfully completed eight years of French in high school and college. I landed a job working for one of the most respected PR agents, Angéla de Bona, who represented the top fashion photographers in the world. Her offices were just off the Champs-Elysées. She was a former model and spoke four languages fluently. On my first day, she asked what language I wanted her to speak to me. I said, "French." She didn't speak one word of English to me until my last day. Looking back, it all took a little time to get used to.

In fact, there were days I felt defeated. Even the computer software programs were different. I wanted to give up. I felt completely isolated, thousands of miles away from the very place I was hell-bent on leaving. One evening, I was at a restaurant in the heart of Paris with a few friends. As our food came, I realized that I needed a fork and completely blanked on the French word for fork. I paid in a harried rush and left the restaurant, tears streaming down my cheeks the entire ride home. The next morning, I jolted out of bed. Here I was, a small-town girl living in Paris working in the fashion industry. I was living the dream. From that day forward, I spoke in French, I dreamed in French, and I didn't shed another tear.

As the holidays approached, the program with Boston University was ending, and it was time to say good-bye to this new life I had created. Angéla asked if I was ready to make the commitment to work full-time in Paris after Christmas and New Year's. I told her that I was heading back to the US with no plans of staying in Paris. It wasn't until the day our airport shuttle came that I realized this dream, this new life I had created, was coming to an end.

As I traveled back the 12 hours from Charles de Gaulle to Boston, then on to Dulles International Airport, it felt like I was moving through quicksand. It wasn't until the last leg of the flight that I realized I was translating the English I was hearing to French. I was warned by friends that the transition back to the States would be hard and that most people wouldn't be able to understand. My friends were right. It wasn't until New Year's Eve that I found my voice again, only in English this time. It would be many more weeks until it hit me that I was back in Gettysburg.

By mid-January, I was back at the Avenue working full-time as I contemplated the next step. My regular customers couldn't wait to catch up on my "fabulous" journeys and experiences. I felt the excitement as I repeated the stories, remembering this incredible experience that forever marked my career.

I distinctly remember this one couple, who had retired to Gettysburg a little over a year before my Paris adventure. They came in once or twice a week, usually for lunch or dinner. I had learned that he was a former editor for the *Washington Post*. "Julie, what is next for you?" he'd ask. I would ramble on about maybe being a journalist or possibly interview with a few folks that Angéla recommended I reach out to.

What was next? I didn't really have a clue. I worked at the Avenue, picked up a second job, and managed to meet friends at the gym in between shifts. In the evenings, I would log on to the Web and search Monster.com for any openings in New York, Philadelphia, or D.C. But nothing happened.

Nearly nine months after I'd returned, I was no closer to a future outside of Gettysburg.

I was acutely aware that for many people, working the family business and earning a little more than $40,000 a year was great as a 22-year-old in 2001. For me though, the struggle to regain my independence was hard. I was able to see my family every day, celebrate the great days, and woefully commiserate on the tough days. Every conversation with my family brought us back to the business, a conversation I couldn't escape.

My parents had successfully built the Avenue into a thriving business and earned the respect of other restaurateurs in the area. I was so incredibly proud to be part of this family—yet I was also terrified that this would be my future.

As if this uncertainty wasn't enough to deal with, September 11, 2001, reminded us all how fragile life could be. It would be many months before I threw myself into a job search again as we waited for the world to adjust to life after 9/11. I focused on working and saving as much money as I could. I managed to pay down my bank loan that supported me when I was abroad and paid off my car in full.

In the spring of 2002, the stress and pressure I had been containing finally reached a critical mass. I panicked my way into seeing a gastroenterologist for what I thought was a life-threatening condition. As my doctor read the results of my colonoscopy (yes, a colonoscopy), he peered over his bifocal lenses and said, "Everything looks great. You are a healthy 22-year-old. My best guess is that you are experiencing all these intestinal issues because of stress. What is causing this?" I shrugged, walked out of the office, got into my car, and cried right there in the parking lot. *I'm fine. It's fine. It's all going to be fine.*

A month after seeing the doctor, I visited a childhood friend who had moved to Conshohocken, which is a suburb of Philadelphia. I gave her all the reasons why I couldn't leave the family business and disappoint my parents. She was worried about me, like good friends do. She called me a few days later and said, "Julie, move in with me and my roommate. We have this room, it's more of a sewing room, but it's a room. You will find a job once you are here." Without hesitation, I said yes.

As I prepared to sell this idea of leaving gainful employment to move to a city, to live in a sewing room, without a job, I could only imagine the reaction I would receive from my parents. I told them over dinner after a particularly grueling summer day at the Avenue. After waiting tables for eight years, I relied on my power of persuasion to sell this move as though it was the opportunity of a lifetime. The sales pitch landed just as I imagined it would. My parents encouraged my sister and me to start our own careers but moving without a job when I had two here in town wasn't viewed as responsible, especially going into the busiest season at the Avenue. But after many conversations, my mind was made up. I never wavered from my choice to leave Gettysburg and the Avenue.

I packed up my belongings, what would fit in my small room, and drove the two hours door-to-door to start my new life in Conshohocken. With a little more than $8,500 in my savings account and no debt, I figured I would be able to live comfortably for the next eight months even if I didn't land a job. I resumed my Monster.com search during the daytime hours when my roommates were at work.

From July to September, I applied to as many jobs as I could in Greater Philadelphia. Most of the positions were in public relations along with a few opportunities to work as a journalist for regional newspapers. With each application, I was hopeful that my experience would be attractive to employers. Having worked in the restaurant for so many years, I was excited to work in a professional environment and put my education to great use.

I finally received a call back for a position as the assistant director to an entrepreneurship institute affiliated with a Philadelphia university. During the interview process, I detailed my experience working in Paris for Angéla, my college degree, and other relevant experiences that I thought would be useful in this position. We spent a great deal of time during those two interviews discussing my background at the Avenue and it became clear that I was offered the position due to my background working to build the family business. It was at this moment that I started to realize the hidden value of what I had learned in that family business and how that differentiated me from the other candidates in consideration for this position.

I graciously accepted the $35,000 per year position. When I shared the news with my family, they too shared in my excitement. We joked that my new salary was $7,000 less than what I'd earned working at the Avenue, waiting tables. Nevertheless, I very much embraced the opportunity to start my professional career.

Working at the Entrepreneurship Institute opened many doors for me professionally. As the assistant director, I was responsible for assisting the executive director with the day-to-day execution of the Institute's initiatives. This included writing press releases, planning our upcoming events, managing the feasibility and business plan competitions, preparing plans for the summer academy, and supporting our entrepreneur-in-residence. I accompanied my boss at regional and local venture events to meet with business leaders across the Greater Philadelphia region.

My boss taught me early on that it was critical to be the first one to arrive and the last one to leave the office and to remain visible. I was to listen first and speak only when I could add real value to the conversation.

We met with powerful business leaders. While obvious that I was young and a female, I was to walk confidently and talk with a purpose so that I didn't get lost in the crowd.

Within one and a half years, I was promoted to associate director at the Institute based on my performance and my contributions to the growth of the Institute. I established a Rolodex that was noteworthy and was invited to co-author an article about women and entrepreneurship that was published in the *Journal for Risk and Financial Management*, a well-respected publication. Things were going very well, and I was feeling good about my prospects.

Not long after this promotion, my boss had an opportunity to serve as the CEO for a start-up and informed me that he would be leaving the Institute. Following his departure, I was not only responsible for moving our main initiatives forward, but I was also given the responsibility of teaching the Entrepreneurship 101 course for the Summer Leadership Academy. The previous summer, I assisted in the creation of the presentations and course plans, but now I would be teaching 20+ rising college freshmen for four weeks that summer.

Then, at the end of the summer, the head of the organization walked into my office for a quick chat. He had never in the nearly two years I had worked here stepped foot on the second floor and certainly not in my office. The meeting started out much like a performance review. I was told that I was doing an incredible job managing the Institute in the absence of a leader. He commended me for my efforts with the Summer Leadership Academy, providing continuity with the program and with the students. A personal visit and a couple of compliments?

But what followed was a tough lesson in humility. He went on to say that they were actively sourcing an executive director for the Institute. "Julie, while we appreciate your hard work, we are specifically looking for an older white male, preferably with a little gray hair. I am sure you understand." I whispered, "What?" He repeated the comment without a second thought. I nodded my head and said, "Okay. Thank you for letting me know."

I was speechless. While I wasn't expecting to be promoted to the executive director's position, I certainly wasn't expecting to hear that they were looking specifically for an older white male to fill the position. That is, in fact, exactly who they recruited for this position. I was given the opportunity to meet with him during the interview process. I was unimpressed with him and the overall experience at this point. Regardless, he was hired.

In the month following his hiring, my day-to-day responsibilities only increased. In effect, I was essentially training my boss. If there was a particular area that he was not familiar with, he would ask me to just add that to my plate since I already had the experience completing these items. He also made sure to ask me to have his coffee prepared in the morning when he arrived.

Rather than give in to angry defeat, I instead focused on developing relationships and expanding my sphere of influence. Out of respect for the Institute, I shared my desire to find a new position with only a few business leaders. They couldn't understand why I would want to leave such a thriving organization, especially one that I had helped build. A managing partner from a small venture fund in the region was excited to hear that I was looking for my next opportunity. He was looking for an executive director.

After a few sidebar conversations, I was invited to the office to be formally interviewed by their board of directors. This venture capital organization assisted early-stage companies, from New England to North Carolina, with securing $1 million to $5 million in funding. In this position, I would be collaborating with venture capitalists, private equity investors, and institutional investors who were seeking early-stage investment opportunities. While this role was certainly a reach goal, the board of directors agreed that I would be a great asset to come on board.

At 26, I had achieved my 10-year plan a few years ahead of schedule.

I provided a two-week notice to my current boss and started to plan my transition to my new position.

On my last day, after a fond farewell from my colleagues, I received a call from the managing partner at the firm I was joining. He asked me to walk out of the building where I could talk. My stomach dropped. What was going on?

Once I was out of range from others in the building, he shared that my current boss had called him and asked that they immediately rescind their offer. My current boss was delivering a message from the head of our organization that I was to remain at the Institute or the relationship between the VC organization and the Institute could become strained. I was speechless. My new boss was furious but reassured me that this was a sign of how valuable I was to the organization.

Later that same day, I was scheduled for a formal exit interview. When asked if I'd like to share any information to be documented in my file, I said I had a few things I'd like to discuss. I detailed the former conversation regarding the search for the executive director and the most recent call to my new employer.

I heard a gasp, followed by "Are you going to sue? Did you retain a lawyer?" I smugly said, "Should I?" After a long silence, instinctively I said, "I don't have intentions to sue. However, I do want to be sure that all of these details are documented in my file for all parties involved. I also would like a full copy of the exit interview for my files." The HR woman thanked me for being so reasonable. At the time, I didn't fully comprehend the severity of these actions. I was more focused on taking the next step in my career in an industry where there are very few women. A lawsuit was not even a consideration. I didn't want this experience to limit my ability in any way to rise in this industry. As naïve as it may sound, I was stepping into a role I had justly earned. I was proud of that.

As it turned out, my proud naivete was short-lived.

The transition to executive director felt natural, yet there were some issues. During my welcome lunch, the marketing coordinator quit, and the previous assistant director explained that she had recently been demoted. Not quite the warm welcome I was expecting. I quickly started the search for a new assistant director and was fortunate to find a talented and driven replacement. In a few short months, we were a well-oiled machine. We streamlined planning and processes, saving thousands of dollars from the bottom line, and continued to deliver against the board's directives and goals. I traveled up and down the East Coast, scored meetings with powerful people, including a top executive at NASDAQ, who told me how impressive I was. I was even featured in the *Philadelphia Business Journal*. Daymond John and Senator Joe Biden, among others, committed to speak at our events.

From the outside looking in, this was a dream job. But on the inside, the reality was a far departure from glamourous. My time here would only last for a little over a year.

During this transition, I actively interviewed for opportunities in D.C. I had met Steve, now my husband of 14 years. He was a recovering New Yorker and an established entrepreneur living in Atlanta, Georgia. It made sense for me to relocate, being that I was looking to transition to a new city.

The transition to Atlanta was absolutely the right personal decision, but it was to some degree professional suicide. The venture capital and private equity community was not as mature in Atlanta in 2006, with little or no opportunities available. Not only was I acclimating to a new city, but I was also learning how to accept the hard reality that my former experience and success were not transferrable.

I was reminded that I could always find a waitressing job to fill in the gaps while I was job searching. Not a helpful reminder, but that notion urged me to press harder in my search.

I pivoted my search to interactive advertising agencies in the Greater Atlanta area and accepted a position as a business development marketing manager, responsible for assisting the business development team and for managing all outward-facing marketing and public relations activities.

My hope with this transition was to rebuild a network of colleagues and continue to grow my experience and capabilities. The agency space was intriguing. We had an HR director who sourced fat-free Cheez-its and stocked the refrigerators with beer. I sat on the Culture Club board for the agency. Fun, right?

This was a far departure from the corporate, Brooks Brothers–suit environment I had just left. I excelled in my role, executed flawlessly, and achieved the goals and objectives the CEO tasked me to do. I did my best to listen, learn, and stay in my lane, as directed by my boss. After two years in this role, it became increasingly clear that I had outgrown the work and the agency.

A competing agency recruited me to develop the strategic practice and lead the strategy team for the agency. Finally, an opportunity to use more of my background and skills. We didn't have a happiness director at this agency, so it normalized the experience. Located in a super hip warehouse district near midtown, I settled in the role and increased my visibility with the management team. The company was going through a growth stage, expanding from 20 employees to over 45 with additional contractors.

My experience working with the family business and assisting early-stage companies cautioned me that this kind of growth was unsustainable. High-cost employees were outpacing the sales funnel. Within less than a year, there were waves of layoffs without notice. The operational processes were less than efficient with little oversight on how billable time was being spent. I survived the downsizing, and because of that I was now expected to do more with little appreciation. It was exhausting.

During this time, Steve and I were married. Because I didn't accrue enough vacation, I was not able to plan a honeymoon until the following spring. My husband, already a successful entrepreneur, was very supportive of my career goals but found some of my agency work stories incredulous. He couldn't believe that modern-day companies tolerated this type of activity. It was at this time I had started to think about running my own business, and I shared with Steve my desire to start my own agency. He encouraged me to start a side hustle to see if I could build revenue before leaving my full-time salary.

A few of my closest colleagues, now friends, at the agency were also interested in starting our own agency. Each of us brought a unique skill set and sense of expertise to the proposed venture. I took on the onus of scheduling meetings after hours to discuss our business plan and approach for starting this business. We had even started thinking through company names and logos. But in the end, our conversations waned as the agency started to downsize and we were all expected to add more value if we wanted to keep our roles. Others on our proposed start-up team also expected to earn $150,000 per year in salaries if they were to step away from their current jobs and launch this venture.

Conversations halted at this stage as a group; however, two of us quietly worked our connections to secure our first client. It was a $25,000 opportunity that would jump-start our new business venture. But alas, during this process, I had discovered that my partner was struggling with substance abuse. Her obvious struggle even led our client to ultimately move on to another agency after our contract was up. I'd be lying if I said that I blamed them. I had the hard discussion with my partner that I needed to focus on my work at the agency and I would table our venture for now. It was my way out, at least for the interim.

Meanwhile, back at my day job, work was picking up and we secured a strategy engagement with a well-respected oil and gas company and the largest global shipping provider. Each engage-ment provided an opportunity to work with C-level executive leadership at both companies. After just three short years, I felt like I was finally making my way back to the level I had reached in Philadelphia.

It was now 2008. The swine flu reached the US and proved to be destructive, affecting more than 60 million people over the course of one year, an early precursor to the global pandemic. On a client trip to Texas, I sat next to a passenger for nearly five hours who coughed as though his lungs were going to burst. This was not how I wanted to start a three-day intensive workshop with over 20 client stakeholders. Despite the rocky start, we began our eight-to-ten-hour days conducting workshops and gathering stakeholder insights to inform our strategy.

By the third day, I suffered with a 102-degree fever. At the end of the day, I asked my boss and colleagues if we were hav-ing a working dinner. "No, we are hitting a rave tonight." For a moment, I thought he was joking. Since this was not a work requirement, I asked for permission to order dinner in and rest. We had another full day ahead of us and then a five-hour plane trip back to Atlanta. My boss responded with "I was expecting you to drive us to the rave." I politely declined and shuffled off to my room.

The next morning, my symptoms were worse. I showered, packed, and met my team in the lobby. As I walked toward the team, I smelled stale beer and cigarettes. Judging from the stench and the wide eyes, they were all recovering from quite the hang-over. My boss mentioned they didn't get home until nearly 5am.

He was icy and short-tempered when he told me that he expected me to lead the meetings all day. I could barely stand, coughed like a heavy smoker, and felt hot to the touch and now I was tasked to lead the day's events?

I wasn't able to. I could barely take a breath without coughing, which made the rest of the room nervous. (Justifiably so.) Once we left the building, I collapsed into the back seat of the car as we drove to the airport. The VP of Client Services shared his concerns as he could tell I was barely holding it together. My boss on the other hand got into the car and immediately started to berate me for my performance. He rattled off a list of items that I was to immediately start working on, including collating the notes from each meeting, putting together a PowerPoint, and developing our recommendations. I mentioned that it was likely I would need to take a sick day being that at this point the swine flu was so volatile and contagious. He scoffed and said that I could take my computer home and work from there if I had to.

The next seven days were hell for me. I was the sickest I had ever been in my life. My 102-degree fever lasted for seven full days. I missed four days of work. My doctor said that I should stay quarantined from others for seven to ten days as it was highly contagious and only if I was unable to drink water, I was to proceed to the ER. My boss sent rapid-fire emails, one right after the other, demanding that I complete my assignments. He copied the CEO on an email stating that he had concerns about my work performance and my complete lack of accountability. The VP of Client Services emailed me separately that he would try to help me as he knew I was terribly ill.

I don't know if it was the fever or a buildup of years of this demeaning management style, but I was furious. Not only was I completely competent in my job role, taking full responsibility and accountability for my work, but I had been placed in a very precarious situation regarding my health. Not to mention, I had to ask permission to not attend a rave with three grown men on a business trip.

That following Tuesday, I dragged myself in to work. I coached myself on keeping calm and focusing on the work that needed to be accomplished. *I'm fine. It's fine. It's all going to be fine.*

As I rounded the corner to my office, I swallowed hard in anticipation of speaking to my boss. I knocked on his door and asked to come in. Maybe it was the fever or quite possibly the smell of cigarettes emanating from his office. I stood in front of his desk, said hello, and followed it by "I wanted to let you know that today will be my last day. I will wrap up the project files that are remaining before the end of the day." And with that, I turned and walked out.

Within minutes, the CEO had requested that I stop in his office. I obliged. He immediately went into an explanation about how my boss was just being his normal self. The CEO valued my contribution to the agency and asked that I reconsider my decision to leave. I took the opportunity to tell the CEO that I respected him and greatly appreciated the opportunities that I had with this agency. I also expressed that this was not a planned decision. I didn't go into work that morning with the intent on quitting. After what felt like an hour, I thanked him and wished him well. He still looked completely baffled at my decision. He said as I walked to the door, "What will you do?" I said, "I don't really know. Maybe I will start my own agency." He smiled smugly and said, "I am sure you will."

An overwhelming sense of relief washed over me as I walked out of the office that day.

CHAPTER THREE

⌒

A MOMENT OF TRUTH

My mind was racing a thousand thoughts per minute as I crossed the parking lot. Did I really just quit my job? It was certainly not my intent to quit. I'd had enough. The smirks, the passive-aggressive behavior, the complete lack of professionalism, all contributed to this moment. I was driven by instinct.

On the drive home, my cell phone rang. It was my dad. My dad was often my first call in situations where I needed reassurance on decisions that I had made. If he didn't call me, I would have called him on the drive home.

"Well, that didn't go as I had hoped," I calmly said. "I literally quit my job." There was a pause, a moment of silence on the other end of the phone. Keenly aware of what had happened on the business trip and in the week following the trip, he said, "Good for you. Now you can focus on what is ahead. Does Steve know?"

The truth was, I failed to discuss this decision with my husband. Steve knew I was unhappy, but we'd never really had a full conversation about me quitting my job. In fact, I had never really considered quitting this job or any job for that matter. That wasn't my style. Steve encouraged me to continue working to earn a solid income while growing my side hustle. As an active contributor to the monthly household expenses, on face value, this was the logical approach.

As I finished the commute home, I was struck by the parallel between my situation and what my dad had endured in the position where he'd dedicated 20 years of his career. The environment, while different than the environments I encountered, was toxic. He worked tirelessly for a company that grossly undervalued his contributions. He traveled nearly 40% of the time in his last five years with the company, spending much of his time in hotels and away from our family. My mom carried the weight of her job, the household, and Marci and me. It was my mom who pushed my dad to take this opportunity to invest in the Avenue. At least with the restaurant, he would be home, even if it meant he would have to work 80 hours a week. However, they discussed it in advance of him leaving his job and becoming an entrepreneur full-time. It seems I missed that part of the lesson.

By the time I reached our house, I still didn't have the words to aptly explain to Steve why I'd made this split-second decision. After work on most days, Steve and I routinely asked each other how the day went. When he asked me how my day went, I mumbled, "Well, I quit my job. I didn't mean to, but I did." Judging from the look on his face, he thought I was joking. "No, seriously. How was your day?" I then explained in detail the events of the day and that this was, in fact, not a joke. His initial response was something like "What will you do? Are you going to look for another job?" These were tough questions to answer.

"I'm going to take the leap of faith and focus on my business full-time..."

Steve nodded, looked me in the eye, and then said, "Good, I support your decision."

A successful businessman himself, Steve instinctively understood the drive to build a business and to do it on your own terms. He started his career on Wall Street, working for a notable investment banking firm. After nearly five years working 80 to 100 hours a week, he made the bold decision to leave New York, move to Atlanta, Georgia, and start his own entrepreneurial ventures.

Steve was incredibly supportive. As an entrepreneur, he knew this was going to be an uphill climb as he'd made the trek so many times before. However, being that it was 2009, the time of the Great Recession, I was faced with another set of challenges.

The ability to make this decision was not lost on me. Most people who want to start a business can't walk away from an income and gainful employment. Most partners wouldn't support a decision to quit because of the smell of stale beer and cigarettes. Most parents wouldn't understand the need or desire to chart a course into the unknown as an entrepreneur.

When I made my decision to walk away from this job, while it seemed like a reflex, I knew it was a calculated risk. Our household would not financially suffer if I quit my job. I was confident in my own capability to earn money, whether in my own business or for another company. I was diligent in saving over the last few years and built up a cash reserve that would allow me to comfortably live for at least a year, longer if I cut back on the extras. I was raised by entrepreneurs. Both my mom and my dad instilled entrepreneurial ideals into me, even if I wasn't aware of it.

Day 1. The alarm went off at 6:30am just as it would on any other regular workday. I watched *The Today Show*, while I sipped on my coffee and ate my breakfast. I showered quickly, got dressed, and walked upstairs to my makeshift office in the spare bedroom. I had selected a nook of the spare bedroom with the best natural light.

As if starting a new job, I set my work schedule for 8am to 5pm, Monday through Friday. I set up my laptop, extended screen, and the printer. I installed bookshelves above the desk for my binders, files, and favorite business books. With my office space neatly organized, I cracked open a fresh notebook and outlined my first to-do list.

- » Write a business plan
- » Decide on the business name
- » Complete the LLC paperwork, including Articles of Organization
- » Go to the bank and open a business bank account
- » Research and apply for a business license
- » Send email to Rolodex alerting them that I have started a new business
- » Schedule 1-3 conference calls or meetings with contacts for business development
- » Develop a website
- » Lunch at 11:30
- » Dinner at 5pm
- » Workout at 5:30pm

Knowing this was an aggressive list to tackle, I included three achievable things that I could cross off the list. Small tasks, often with no correlation to the business, that could be accomplished to help keep a positive mindset, especially on long workdays and in arduous years. The discipline of completing easy tasks provided encouragement. I maintain this same approach to my to-do list even after nearly 15 years as an entrepreneur. Working through easy and small tasks allows me to physically cross off an item on my list, providing motivation to tackle the bigger items on the list.

Good resources are critical to the foundation of your business. Having a strong background working for entrepreneurial parents and assisting early-stage companies was valuable to me in the start-up process. Look for online resources that provide templates or start-up guides to embarking on this journey. You will find these resources essential to developing your initial to-do list and starting the process. Don't sidestep this process; there are no shortcuts. My early career at the Institute and then at the VC organization taught me the value of developing a business plan. I reviewed and critiqued well over 1,000 business plans across industry to include life sciences, biotech, technology, professional services, and retail, among others. I vetted those business plans before making recommendations as to whether the company should be presented at our regional venture conferences. I remember viewing a business plan for a company looking to place video kiosks on college campuses. College students could rent a DVD -remember this is the early 2000s—for as little as $1. During our review session, most of the investors laughed at the idea that people would rent a DVD from a kiosk. A great lesson in humility. We certainly misread that opportunity, but it wasn't a well-written business plan. These experiences gave me an advantage in that I knew what it felt like to be on the other side of the table.

As I taught in the Business Leadership Academy, a business plan is a living, breathing document that is meant to be updated and adapted as the business grows. I downloaded a business plan template as a guideline and started the process of moving from section to section. Despite my expertise, I found myself staring at the blank screen for what felt like hours. I tackled what I felt were the easiest sections first to get into a rhythm. If I got stuck, I moved on and revisited the section with fresh eyes the next morning.

I found the process of writing a business plan to be ironic. I mean, I had literally taught dozens of young entrepreneurs how to go through this process of writing business plans, and I had even graded their attempts! And now, here I was, faced with the very same task, and I must confess that it wasn't an easy chore. Remember, a business plan is the fundamental compass for your company's purpose and overall direction. It takes some real thought and time to pinpoint all of this, and then to write it down in a concise and meaningful way.

For many new entrepreneurs, the hurdle of writing a business plan is often hard to overcome. I was fortunate in that I had this valuable career experience. This is a critical step. If you can't articulate who you are, what you do, and how it will drive value, then it will be even more difficult to sell anyone on your products and services. Don't rush the process either. Revisit your business plan quarterly and adapt based on the feedback you've received or changes in your business model. Look for free online business plan templates at www.score.org. You can also do a simple search on Google to find free templates and checklists for starting a business. As part of this process, I carefully and thoughtfully developed my "why" for my elevator pitch. An elevator pitch is essentially a 30-to-60-second presentation on the business, what you do, and why you do it. The concept is that if you ride an elevator with a person, you should be able to deliver this presentation in the time it takes to go from the bottom floor to the top of the building. I wrote, practiced aloud, edited, practiced again, and edited for hours. I wish I had recorded those early presentations as a reminder of where it all began. With the pitch perfected, I was even more excited about the future of the business.

But looking back, I now realize that in addition to all the work and effort I put into polishing my elevator pitch, I should have practiced it on some friends and colleagues. That would have been most helpful.

My next task was to set up an account at Wells Fargo, which proved to be another "learning opportunity." I scheduled a meeting with the business banker to go over setting up a business account, but as it turned out, I was completely unprepared. For someone who was trying to present herself as a business professional, it was very awkward. The banker asked for my Operating Agreement and LLC documentation, as well as a bunch of other documents that I had not brought to the appointment. I had to apologize profusely, then go back to my office, gather all the remaining documentation, and schedule a follow-up appointment to set up the business account. I should have known better. I built checklists for entrepreneurs in the past. I was successful on the second meeting with the banker. But it was clearly a clumsy start. During that second meeting, he inquired about the business and how things were going.

Taking advantage of this opportunity to deliver my newly minted elevator pitch, I delivered it to him confidently. "Junction Creative Solutions combines the intellectual capital of a traditional business consulting firm with the creative execution of an ad agency. As a strategic firm, we take a results-driven approach to establish and grow your business." He acknowledged me with a nod, but I knew he had no idea what I was talking about. I should have immediately recognized that this was a not good sign.

Junction Creative was founded on the notion that it was the intersection between strategy and execution, designed to assist clients in developing the right strategies yet also provide a clear executable road map for success. It's also the inspiration for the name of the business. I wanted to be a resource for clients looking to grow their business, whether a start-up company or a growth-stage company. Our tagline: "Strategy. Impact. Results." I wanted our clients to rely on us not only for the big thinking but also for rolling our sleeves up and getting the work done. A concept, unfortunately, that required a lot of explanation to potential clients in the early days.

I found that explaining my "why" was the "aha" moment for prospective clients when given in the context of what motivated me to start the business. While my elevator introduction sounded great with the right balance of buzzwords, the concept was lost on most people. When met with blanks stares or furrowed brows, I would simply talk through the path that led me to launch this business.

In my experience both working with early-stage companies and as a strategist at interactive advertising agencies, I saw an opportunity to blend critical business thinking with marketing execution to deliver revenue for our clients. Junction was a solution for companies who were tired of working with agencies who were solely focused on billable rate and "big idea" creative. We focused on thinking through the business challenges and presenting solutions designed to mitigate those risks and drive real value. Success is in the execution.

I started my own business to be a solution to companies who were looking for an agency partner who was accountable, transparent, and focused on the bottom line. The client's bottom line, not the agency's.

Over the next two weeks, I challenged myself to reach out to my former colleagues, contacts in my Rolodex, and my friends to share the news that I was officially open for business. I started with my friends, some who had known me since I was four years old, others who I had met in college, Philadelphia, and now Atlanta. They offered words of encouragement and proved to be a soft shoulder to cry on when I was feeling a little out of sorts.

For someone who has been in high-pressure work environments and had spoken in front of crowds of 500 people, I was surprised by how vulnerable I felt placing phone calls or having coffee with some of my most trusted friends and family. Before each call, I would practice out loud in front of a mirror. I wanted to appear confident and sure of myself. It was as if I was selling them on why I made this incredibly risky life decision to become an entrepreneur during what was deemed as the worst economic climate of the last century. I dug deep and channeled my inner waitress who could sell a hot fudge brownie sundae to a customer after they'd finished appetizers, an entrée, and a basket of rolls. I could sell this!

One of my first calls was to a great friend from college, who had started his business while we were still in college. When I was working in Philadelphia, I hired Bill and his company and did what I could to introduce him to people that were looking for his services. When I called to tell him that I was branching out on my own, Bill shared his own experiences, the good and the bad, but always with a healthy dose of optimism. He said that when I was ready, he would be happy to build my first website. I would take him up on the offer to make it official online.

This friendship evolved into a partnership between our companies. We became referral partners sending opportunities to each other and often sharing clients. We talked about our experiences, processes, and methodologies and commiserated on the challenging moments that we faced. This partnership and friendship stood the test of time as we continue to partner to the present day. Partners like this are hard to come by. I appreciate this partnership for what it has taught me about business and relationships.

I called my lifelong friends, a small group of accomplished women in their respective fields, who shared nearly every journey with me since childhood. Their support was unconditional.

Having known me as long as they had, they weren't surprised by my decision. I didn't dare tell them how scared I was, but they knew exactly what to say when I needed it the most.

Telling my family and extended family was encouraging. I grew up in a family that was very close to our uncles, aunts, cousins, second cousins, etc. With nine of us all born within a year of each other, we were raised like siblings. Our family came from a long line of small business entrepreneurs. My maternal grandparents owned gas stations and convenience stores. My mom started her own hair salon in her early 20s. My paternal grandfather was in corporate sales but eventually opened a toy store. One uncle owned a landscaping business and nursery, a great-aunt and uncle owned a flower shop, and another aunt and uncle owned a cattle farm. I was raised to understand what it took to be successful. I listened and learned, asking them questions about sales, hiring people, etc.

Before reaching out to my Rolodex, I reached out to Jeff, a friend and former colleague who I worked with at both agencies in Atlanta; he was one of my first phone calls. He had left the agency space just before I did and was now killing it at IBM. He too shared his support and even made an introduction that led to one of my very first clients. As the years pass, we try to meet on a regular basis for lunch to catch up, vent, and provide encouragement to each other.

My dream of becoming an entrepreneur was now my reality—or so I thought. Initially feeling energized by my friends' and family's unwavering support, I gained enough confidence to call those very important people I had in my Rolodex. But this process proved to be a most sobering experience. Respectful of each's time and position, I sent an initial email requesting 15 to 30 minutes of their time. I scheduled these meetings through their respective administrators and/or managed to catch them on the evening commute.

While most were receptive to a call, I was surprised and disappointed by each conversation and how unproductive they were. As we caught up on what was happening with their business, I shared how I had finally decided to start my own firm. After silent pauses, I would hear "oh, that's cute" or "interesting" or "sounds great." Many asked if I was looking for a job. A few thought I was pitching my services and directly said that they don't work with companies that don't have a proven track record of success. I idolized many of these entrepreneurs and colleagues during my start in Philadelphia. I earned their respect by working hard and executing. But this was a setback for sure. Much like the dread of rebuilding my career in Atlanta, I was faced with a similar experience. I was unproven as an entrepreneur with a new business.

When my dad quit his job, after a successful 20 years under his belt, I believe his boss's words were "Mark, you have lost your mind." This was from someone who he respected and considered a friend. Instead of encouragement, my dad was greeted with apprehension. Even worse, there were other "friends" who didn't show up to support my parents on the first day or even in the 10 years they owned the Avenue. This would be a topic of conversation during our family dinners. Growing up in a small town, it was difficult to dodge the rumors. The disappointment was real. It was hard to watch this kind of impact it had on my parents, my sister, and me. While it didn't stop my parents from achieving success at the Avenue, I knew that it stung.

This lesson in disappointment was tough to learn this early in my journey, forcing me to accept that I was starting a new and perhaps rocky chapter in my career. You will remember the people who support you unconditionally. Thank them often and always return the encouragement wherever their journey takes them. You will continue to face disappointment that is hard to overcome, but trust that it is part of any entrepreneurial journey. It builds character and strengthens your resolve.

As I moved through the first year, I secured my first clients to add to my portfolio. The total value of those customers was less than $35,000 and certainly only accounted for less than 150 hours of my time. I had expanded my sphere of influence to now include other colleagues who started their own website development shops or complementary professional services. In many situations, I used resources in my extended network to assist with completing projects that fell outside of my skill set. It wasn't a perfect process but, in the end, we delivered successfully for each client.

The financial aspect of working with new clients was great. I was officially earning money for my efforts, albeit drastically less than what I had become accustomed to. It reminded me of when I accepted the position at the Institute, earning $7,000 less than

I did as a full-time waitress. It encouraged me to set my sights higher to reach the next revenue plateau.

Reaching my first year in business should have been a milestone to celebrate. Building this business was hard. My personality has always been a "my glass is always full" approach to life. This year had truly challenged me emotionally and physically. Most nights I was restless, unable to get sound sleep, worrying about the next day, the next deal, and how much longer I could continue at this frantic pace. I was doing all the jobs I needed to do. I was CEO, sales representative, strategist, project manager, content writer, and janitor. While I would maintain my positive outlook around others, I would retire to my nook in the spare bedroom and allow myself to be angry, frustrated, or sad. This was, to this point, one of the hardest chapters in my life.

It was now May 2011, nearly 18 months since I started Junction; I was fearful that my dedication and hard work were not destined for success. It was then that I started to feel real fear. There was just no business coming in.

Fear comes in various forms. I remember climbing the Eiffel Tower to Level 2 when I lived in Paris. The walk up was a breeze. Coming down the stairs, which were transparent, and you could literally see nearly 400 feet straight down to the ground, was terrifying to me. I remember sitting on the stairs, near tears at the thought of having to walk the entire way down. At a certain point in the descent, I just focused on one slow step at a time, not allowing my eyes to wander to the depths below.

Starting a business was a different kind of fear, the kind that is mixed with uncertainty and doubt. Would I be able to start again? Would I be successful? What would happen if I failed at this? When will the revenue support the growth? Did I make a mistake? Who do I think I am? Whose idea was this anyway? *It's fine. I'm fine. It's going to be fine.*

I tried to keep the negative thoughts out of my mind. The simple truth is that there will be days when you feel worthless and a shell of your former self. Even when questioned by others as to how things were going, I always replied positively that the business was growing and shared the most recent opportunities. The truth was not exactly as upbeat as I presented, but people don't want to hear about your self-doubt; after all this is a path that you have chosen voluntarily in order to live the American dream.

Then, after losing three potential clients, largely due to my company being a start-up, and with only a few small business clients in my portfolio, I was frustrated. I cried. I screamed. I was down to the last $4,500 in my savings account. In those moments, I questioned every single decision from my first job to starting this business.

In early June, one of my partners reached out to schedule a coffee with a contact he'd made. He was meeting with the senior vice president at Yahoo! to discuss agency needs. He invited me to join as he thought I was better at managing a sales pitch. I accepted the invitation. What did I have to lose at this point? But in truth, I really didn't have much expectation.

But surprisingly, the meeting went well and led to subsequent meetings to discuss immediate needs. With the economy in deep decline at that time, the company was scrambling to maximize budgets and provide more return on investment to its advertisers.

I conducted a mini-strategy session to better understand the current needs and agency resources. The current agency was billing 20 resources against this budget, missed 50% of the deadlines, and put added pressure on the company's marketing team. I outlined a strategy to streamline communications between the company and the agency and implemented a process to drive efficiency. Skeptical of our ability to execute, I asked for 30 days. If in 30 days, I could show them the value, I wanted a Master Services Agreement for this nearly seven-figure opportunity in the first year.

As luck would have it, my sister Marci had recently left her position as a mechanical engineer after surviving the same toxic environment that my dad had endured for 20 years. She visited Atlanta to take a break. She was with me when I received the phone call with the green light to move forward on the 30 days!

As soon as the shock wore off, I had the realization that I was employee number one with a handful of contractors to help assist with projects. I begged Marci to stay for two weeks. Since she had time and wasn't sure what her next move was, she could help me get the operations set up and earn money at the same time. We convinced our contractors to join in the 30-day challenge. We were about to find out how 4.5 people could complete the work of 20 people, in 30 days. If Marci could build custom elevators that run in some of the most notable skyscrapers in the United States, surely she could organize our team?

And we did just that. Blood, sweat, no sleep, tears, four-letter expletives and all, we made it look easy for those 30 days. Without question, we achieved our MSA status and signed our first contract with one of the largest content platforms on the Web.

Proven track record, yes, I do believe so. And we were just getting started.

As I listened to the "way to go, girls" and the "you're so lucky" reactions from others, I asked myself if it was really luck. I believe it was a result of my hard work and design that prepared me to take advantage of this incredible opportunity. I spent the better part of a year developing trusted relationships with other business owners. I didn't sleep, fraught with worry. I showed up every day and put in the work, even though it felt like I was just marking time. It was all part of this process. I had to reframe what being an entrepreneur meant. I had to let go of the idea of being comfortable and complacent. It prepared me for the moment I wasn't expecting. The door opened. I was prepared and ready to rock and roll.

As an entrepreneur, you will learn that the highs are so high, but the lows are lower than you thought possible. Embrace those dark moments, feel the unfulfilled feelings, and understand that the emotions are real. And then get back to work.

IMPORTANT DETAILS

- » Take every opportunity to learn from the people or the environment around you.
- » Understand that you will always be your best advocate.
- » Sometimes, stepping outside of your comfort zone presents real opportunities that you did not plan.

CHAPTER FOUR

DEALING WITH MONEY AS A START-UP

There is nothing more satisfying than being able to earn revenue for your business, regardless of the amount. I have never worked with an entrepreneur or consulted with a business owner who wasn't interested in making money. After all, financial freedom is one of the greatest outcomes of starting and growing a business. I was no different.

What is not taught in classrooms, seminars, or business books is the core fundamentals of money management. I am not talking about just balancing your checkbook (although helpful). I am referring to the process of funding the business, earning money to support the business, effectively managing the money you do have, and learning how to apply the money in order to grow. This will happen in this order—always—and you cannot skip a step.

Regardless of whether you have a service or product-based business, it takes an unwavering belief in your ability to convince customers to purchase those goods or services. In my case, Junction allowed me to offer services that I, myself, had provided for more than 10 years, to hundreds of companies, including global Fortune 1000 brands.

I made the decision to boot-strap my own business, leveraging my personal savings to fund the operations, sales, marketing, and contract freelance employees who worked with me. My husband, Steve, was not a stranger to building businesses from the ground up. And he generously offered to give me financial support to start the business. Even though I was desperate and stressed at times, I declined his offer. It was a difficult decision, but the best one I've made.

I didn't want my story to start with "my husband funded my business," especially since many people in my social circle assumed that he did. I was determined to prove that I could earn my way in this business, even if it meant a lot of sacrifice and sleepless nights.

I know that not all entrepreneurs will be able to self-fund their business. You can choose to raise funding from a venture capital firm, private equity, small business loan, or family, friends, and others. It's critically important to understand the expectations that come with taking "other people's money." Don't let the money that they invest in your firm fool you into thinking that you will be an overnight success. The process is the same whether you are putting your savings to work or being funded by a third party.

When I drafted my business plan, I set a realistic and reachable revenue goal for Junction. I assumed that it would take about 12 months to achieve the realistic revenue goal. When I failed to hit the revenue goal in the first year, I was crushed. It was hard to remind myself to not let the missed expectations overshadow the dream.

Accept the fact that there are no shortcuts. I am asked often, "if you could give a new entrepreneur a piece of advice, what would it be?" My advice is that it takes a minimum of 18 to 24 months to get a business launched and to become profitable. Set that as the expectation. Starting a business is hard enough without carrying the emotional weight of missed expectations.

In my career, I have consulted with hundreds and hundreds of entrepreneurs. I've sat through all sorts of PowerPoint presentations and sifted through financial projections. With each review, I would always ask the entrepreneur: "How do you plan to earn the money to support these projections?" I would receive a litany of responses, my favorite being "please refer to the financial projections." While developing financial projections is an important part of starting a business, I would suggest you concentrate more of your focus on *how* you plan to earn money. If you don't know how to earn real revenue, the "financial projections" are only as valuable as the paper they are printed on.

In the late 90s, the minimum wage for a waitress was three dollars and 12 cents per hour. I remember seeing my first pay stub and thinking this had to be incorrect. After putting in long shifts for two weeks, I would earn only $80 after taxes. The silver lining was, of course, the ability to earn cash tips each shift. If I was lucky, I could earn anywhere from $60 to $120 in tips depending on the shift (breakfast, lunch, or dinner).

The Avenue had built a great number of customers, whether locals or tourists, who came into the restaurant weekly, monthly, or on their annual trip to Gettysburg. Over the years, you knew which customers tipped generously and also the few who left only a quarter or 50 cents. Other waitresses would grumble and huff if they had to serve the 50-cent customer. I didn't mind so much—because on those slow winter shifts, the 50-cent tips added up to something. January was one of the slowest months in the restaurant, with no tourists to speak of and snow that kept locals from coming in. It was not unheard of to work an eight-hour shift and go home with only $4.50.

My overall point regarding revenue? Expect nothing. It will shield you from disappointment so that what you do achieve is an unexpected reward. In the restaurant, I waited for those unexpected rewards. The returning families who would request for me to serve their table, chat with me, linger after dinner, and leave a crisp 10-dollar bill or a 20-dollar bill even if that was well above the standard gratuity percentage—those were the unexpected rewards I loved.

I credit my experience as a waitress in providing a solid foundation in understanding just how hard it is to earn money. You start each day with zero dollars in your pocket. The financial success of your shift depends on your ability to provide exceptional service and to upsell with appetizers or desserts. In my quest to be crowned the best waitress at the Avenue, I would compete with Ryan, a waiter who was also very popular with the diners. I'll never forget on one of the busiest summer days, he and I went head-to-head on a 10-hour shift. We sold omelets, steak and eggs, hot turkey sandwiches, roasted chicken, seafood platters, steaks, milkshakes, and hot fudge brownie sundaes. And just when I thought I couldn't serve another round of refills, I would look across the dining room and see Ryan zipping around with a smile on his face.

My dad will tell you that it was pure magic watching the two of us run the dining room. Dad couldn't believe that a simple bet to see who would be named the best waitress/waiter at the Avenue meant record sales. As it turned out, Ryan and I ended up with the same amount in food sales. Our tips became the deciding factor. And I clinched victory with a $20 tip at the end of the evening, surpassing Ryan by less than five dollars. Counting my money at the end of that shift was an incredible feeling. I made more that day than any other day waitressing at the Avenue.

If not for this experience waiting tables, I don't know that I would have weathered the long months when I was chasing any and all projects I could find at Junction. It didn't matter if the project was $500 or $10,000. The biggest difference is that at the Avenue, my parents carried the weight of attracting new customers, who would become loyal to our business as frequent diners. But as Employee Number 1 at Junction, I was now aware that if I wanted to generate revenue, I was responsible for earning it.

From my very first contract to eventually winning a Fortune 1000 deal, I understood the value of each dollar and knew just how hard it was to earn each one. Even now, I fully appreciate that our clients entrust their marketing dollars with my firm, whether a small business with a limited budget or an enterprise-level client with robust marketing budgets. Having earned every dollar over the last 15 years, I never take a single dollar for granted.

As my business gradually gained momentum, I was now faced with the new challenges with how to effectively manage the cash flowing into the business. The original concerns of self-doubt of how to make money would be replaced with an entirely new set of worries to think through during those sleepless nights.

That is, who do I need to hire? Will I add 1099 contract employees? Will I keep partnering with other firms and pay a slightly higher billable hour? Do we have the right software and technology to support the account? How many computers do we need to purchase? How much should I invest in ongoing marketing for the firm? What if a client doesn't renew? Do I need a physical office? What is our total monthly liability versus our monthly income?

Before finally beginning to earn an abundance of money, I first learned how to operate on a very lean budget. I worked from a small office in my home: it was the in-law suite in the basement of our house. I used an old laptop that was originally given to me as a Christmas present. I limited expenses to only those items that I truly needed to support the day-to-day function of the business. I drafted my own invoices using templates found in Microsoft Word. If I met with new partners or clients, I would be sure to list and expense meals and mileage. In those first 18 months, I was able to simply track any and all revenue and expenses on a single spreadsheet. I watched every entry on that spreadsheet like a hawk.

Bit by bit, as there was a general infusion of cash flow into the business, it became more and more clear to me that I lacked a plan—a real financial plan. So, I hired the best part-time accounting manager I knew, more fondly known as my mom. She had opened her own business at the age of 21, successfully managed our family's finances for decades, built a 20-year career at the local bank, and had worked in lockstep with my dad at the Avenue. I credit her for teaching me, even at a young age, how to make money stretch. She demonstrated how to get all the things that you needed and, if you were lucky, still have enough left over for a few things that you wanted. If there was anyone who could hold me accountable on the finances, it would be she. And I also knew Mom could balance a set of financial books to the penny.

In the early years at the Avenue, the restaurant didn't have a POS (point-of-sale) computer system that managed customer orders and printed receipts. (Remember, this was the mid- to late 1990s, before technology exploded in this industry.) On our busiest days, we could turn one table anywhere from 10 to 14 times. A waitress in one station could serve 40 to 50 tables. At the time, we would take orders on a Carbon Check Receipt Book. We'd write the order, send the ticket to the kitchen, and manually add up the pricing to each line item on the check. We had a standard calculator in the corner where we would all fight to add the subtotal, add 6% sales tax, and then total the bill. Customers took this bill to the register to pay, and we kept the receipt on a spindle next to the register.

During one of our family dinners at the pizza place, my dad lamented that the numbers just weren't adding up. On our busiest day, the register didn't reflect what he felt it should, based on the number of customers and food that we'd served that day. He just had a strong sense that the math wasn't adding up correctly.

As a result of Dad's hunch, my mom, Dad, my sister Marci, and I found ourselves sitting around the family living room with a stack of receipts, a calculator, and a highlighter. We'd cheer when we found an error or discovered a rounding error or a missed charge. But after going through a small stack, the cheers became groans as the amount totaled up to nearly $2,000 missed in one week, with just one of the eight waitresses making $475 errors in one weekend shift. On some tickets, the waitress forgot to list the price of an entire meal or forgot to charge for drinks. Others forgot to tabulate the sales tax correctly or didn't charge it at all. In one or two instances, waitresses were giving family members free appetizers or desserts, assuming it would go unnoticed. It was a mix of error and also dishonesty. (Fortunately, on my own tickets, my discrepancies fell under five dollars.) There is no telling how much this cost the business in our first 18 months at the Avenue.

From that day on, my mom and I took turns going through checks each night until we had implemented a POS system. We did implement a new policy such that after an initial 10-day period, if a waitress failed to charge customers or didn't total the checks properly, the loss was taken from their individual paychecks. Within a short period of time, my audit didn't turn up any mistakes.

A valuable lesson in following the numbers—do it meticulously. One could argue this is a standard challenge in any restaurant, but I would argue that it happens in every business. When money is involved, you must pay close attention to numbers in and numbers out on a daily basis, if that is what it takes.

With Junction, my mom and I quickly set up some critical processes to manage QuickBooks, to establish business payroll accounts, and to distribute electronic invoices. We had an accounting system in place that would allow me to have a real-time snapshot of where the business was financially, whether it was outstanding invoices or cash in the bank. Unlike the first 18 months, I needed the added support of an expert in finance and accounting, as the numbers could not simply be managed on one spreadsheet. I was hopeful that our new system would provide greater visibility for the business 60 days, 90 days, and six months out.

I implemented a system of checks and balances for those processes to ensure that I wouldn't lose sight of the numbers, as the business grew. I log in to the business bank accounts literally every day to do a spot check of the balances. I check the corporate credit cards at least once a week. I compare this against our QuickBooks account, just to be sure the math is adding up correctly. Trust but verify.

I was lucky to be able to trust my mom, who I knew was experienced in handling the business finances. You will need to identify an expert who can assist you with managing the finances. Look for someone that has not only had experience with accounting reconciliation but someone who also understands the needs of a business owner. When my mom retired, I had to find someone that I could trust with my business. Ask colleagues. Do a search on LinkedIn. Or you can inquire for recommendations from QuickBooks or financial management software. You can search by geographic location if you'd like someone on-site at your business or in the same state.

Even when you build a trusted relationship with your accounting team, continue to review the numbers on a regular basis to ensure that the numbers add up. Don't ever just trust what is presented to you. I still continue to check the accounts and charges. In just two months, I discovered a $25,000 discrepancy in the invoices. We underbilled clients. Had I not been looking, we may not have caught it until it was too late. I can't stress enough the need to trust but verify.

With the financial systems in place, I focused on determining what employees or contractors I needed to support our client accounts. Fortunately, Marci was amenable to joining Junction full-time as our director of operations and project management lead. Trained as a mechanical engineer, she had won numerous awards in her career for outperforming and outpacing her colleagues. She was able to take our project management software and establish core operational processes from the initial client kickoff to the completion of the final deliverables.

But know this: Any good process is painstaking to learn and to adopt and to become habit. Real operational process will inform key financial decisions. I learned how valuable it was to understand not only how the work was getting done but how long it took to accomplish each task.

In a few short months, we now knew exactly how many hours it took to deliver each asset. This enabled us to estimate each project properly and then to track the project down to the quarter hour. This would prove to be the critical difference between profit and loss. Don't skip this part.

With a strong understanding of our financials and our processes, we were able to determine how many employees we needed to add to the team. A helpful hint in hiring employees is a simple formula. One full-time employee represents 2,000 working hours in a calendar year (give or take lunches, vacations, breaks, holidays, etc.). For example, if you allocate 1,000 hours per month on client work, it requires roughly five full-time people to deliver on the 1,000 hours each month.

Knowing that our largest account represented 80% of our revenue, at that time, I was hesitant to take on full-time employees until I had at least six months visibility on a particular position. As a result, I continued to use partner resources and outside contractors until I felt very, very confident that our main account could support a long-term role in the business. Only at that point did I start to feel comfortable with the idea of hiring a full-time employee. After all, when you hire someone to join your company, you are now basically saying that you will definitely be able to pay them on a regular and consistent basis. That's quite a promise, e.g., to pay them a salary.

Speaking of salary, every entrepreneur wants to know when and how they should pay themselves. I was no different.

I found that if I was diligent with Junction's business expenses, including payroll, and followed the financial processes we had established, my profit margins would be healthy enough for me to earn a good salary, a salary comparable to the one I had in my last full-time corporate position. Or would it?

I struggled with this. How do you balance paying yourself as the business owner, yet balance the books so that you still have enough cash to float the business if it's unexpectedly needed? This decision gnawed at me, and especially the idea of taking a comparable salary. So, I didn't. Instead, I continued to rely upon my hard-earned life savings if I found I needed to draw some cash. But I did something else to help "reward" my efforts.

For the first few years, instead of drawing a salary, I would take a distribution at the end of the year, solely based on profits that we'd earned that year. I focused on growing revenue for 12 months, so that I could reap the rewards at the end of the year with a kind of a bonus.

For the most part, this worked well. But I would also learn it could be a slippery slope as well. When we had a downturn in the business in year five and year six, I didn't take a dime out of the business as there was not enough profit at the end of those years.

After year six, I came to the conclusion that I needed to pay myself on a consistent basis. I started taking a small salary (less than $40,000 per year in case you are curious) and also a "bonus" distribution at the end of the year.

For many entrepreneurs, making less than $40,000 a year as the CEO might seem ridiculous. The expectation of an executive-level salary is tough to overlook. For me, I was able to budget my personal finances so that a nominal salary can sustain me until I get the larger payout at the end of the year. I've worked with a lot of entrepreneurs who expected six-figure salaries for themselves right at the start yet couldn't pay their employees. I've witnessed investors infuse cash into start-ups, only to pay executive-level salaries, whether or not the business was a success.

But for me, I found my cautious approach held me accountable to myself, my employees, and to the business.

My livelihood is at stake if I mismanage our revenue or waste valuable operational dollars on items that don't positively affect the business. I didn't race to find a new office space; the in-law suite in the basement fit six of us comfortably. I didn't buy Apple computers but rather opted for more cost-effective PCs. I bought our office furniture from OfficeMax and décor from Home Goods. I know where every dollar has been spent. More importantly, I know how much money I have saved in a reserve account.

At a young age, my parents taught me the value of saving money. "Save at least ten percent each pay period to be sure that you will have enough money in the event of an emergency. Make sure to have a four-to-six-month cash reserve." In business, especially in the early years, I'd be lying if I said I had four to six months of operating capital in the bank. However, it became a standard rule that I implemented so that I don't repeat the mistakes of year five and year six. With the money that I was able to save, I could forecast what investments I needed to make regarding infrastructure, technology, people, and growth at the end of the year. Invest only what is required and only that which you can afford.

In 2013, I was invited to speak in New York City on a panel with the chief marketing officers (CMOs) and leadership at some of the most well-respected financial institutions. I was so excited and honored to participate at an event and share a panel with leaders in the financial marketing industry. My firm was being represented at an event that was certain to increase our brand reputation and potentially garner us new business opportunities. Marci accompanied me on the trip to network with the group and provide a sounding board as I prepared for the speaking engagement.

We arrived at the Ritz-Carlton for the session and panel presentation. Despite my nerves, I participated in a great dialogue with leaders on how changes in customer behavior and digital was transforming financial services approach to marketing. After many handshakes and business card exchanges, I told Marci that we were going to have lunch at the Ritz before heading to the airport. While lunch at the Ritz was not typically an approved budget expense, today we would celebrate this milestone for Junction and me.

As our overly priced lunch was delivered, I received a call from our main point of contact at Yahoo!. I immediately picked up the call, hoping that our team had not missed a deliverable while we were in NYC. She was apologetic for reaching me at lunch, sounding almost exasperated. She quickly explained that the new CEO at Yahoo! was terminating all current Master Services Agreement contracts as the company evaluated whether or not internal resources could handle the workload. Unfortunately, I was the only vendor that had a 90-day termination notification, so I was the first agency to receive notice. (As a reference, most mature agencies carried an annual agreement with little or no ability to terminate. I was more agreeable on the terms as I wanted to secure this account for my business nearly three years before.) She apologized and offered her gratitude for being instrumental in achieving their goals and objectives, unlike the previous agency.

As she spoke, I remained calm with a smile on my face. Marci was sitting directly across from me with a look of bewilderment. Without needing a mirror, I knew that the color was draining from my face. It was like being punched in the gut, as I sat celebrating our success being recognized at this marketing event. As I thanked her for the call, I hung up and put the phone down.

"What happened? Did we miss something?" Marci asked.

"Well, do you want the good news or the bad news?" I asked. "The bad news is they are pausing any agency contracts as part of their internal company audit. The good news is I have 90 days to figure out how to replace the revenue. Guess we better enjoy our lunch at the Ritz."

We stared at each other for what felt like an hour, nibbling on French fries. Marci and I still talk to this day about that lunch at the Ritz. It makes us sick to our stomachs just thinking about that afternoon and how unforgiving business can be sometimes.

I'm fine. It's fine. It will all be fine?

This was a defining moment for the business and for me as an entrepreneur. Losing this account was my biggest fear, being that it represented nearly 80% of our annual revenue. It kept me up most nights. And now that it had in fact actually happened, I had to face the feeling of potentially failing. I allowed myself to be upset about it during the lunch at the Ritz. As soon as I got on the airplane, I started to follow up with new contacts from the trip, prospective clients, and current clients to identify any opportunities for new projects. I emailed my colleagues, part-ners, friends, and anyone I had met at industry events. The clock was ticking—I had less than 90 days to make up the revenue or I would have to consider adjustments to the team.

Fortunately, I was responsible with the revenue and the busi-ness savings. I had enough reserve to carry the entire team at the current rate for at least seven months, longer if I needed to make a reduction to the team. We still had 90 days of revenue from this client that would carry us another six months. I didn't have time to be upset or angry. I remained focused on the goal. In just under four months, I was able to replace 80% of the lost revenue.

Revenue is not predictable and certainly not guaranteed. While legal agreements can protect the business against nonpay-ment or renewals, no contract is bulletproof. Without having a system in place to protect the business, my journey as a business owner could have easily gone down a different path. Building a solid foundation around financial management for the business is incredibly important. You don't have to be a financial wizard to understand the core fundamentals, but you do need to understand how you will earn, manage, and invest in growth for the business. Get comfortable with those unexpected gifts and missed expec-tations. I would be lying if I said that managing financial plans and expectations was easy. I still find it difficult even after more than a decade as an entrepreneur.

IMPORTANT DETAILS

» Whether self-funding the business or receiving external investment, always track every single dollar and treat it as if it were your last.

» Trust but always verify. Find people who you can trust to assist in managing your money but always verify the numbers.

» Success isn't in the numbers; rather, it's in the ability to put the numbers on the page.

CHAPTER FIVE

⌐⌐

DEVELOPING ONE'S MANAGEMENT STYLE

At the Avenue, while still a teenager, I was unexpectedly thrust into a role of becoming a manager one summer. My dad had suffered a neck injury that required immediate spine surgery. Because of the severity of the injury, my dad would not be able to drive for six to eight weeks and under no circumstance was he to go into the restaurant. One slip and he could be paralyzed from the neck down. We met for another memorable family meeting to go over the game plan.

Our thought was to focus on just keeping things operating as smoothly as possible. My mom was still working full-time at the bank. She would go to work, stop by the house to check on my dad, and then come into the restaurant to complete the books and drop off the deposits around closing. Marci and I were to split the rest of the time so that one of us was always present in the restaurant. This would sometimes mean waitressing for eight hours and then working as a hostess on another shift. My dad and mom laid out their concerns for the team—who did we need to keep an eye on, did we have all of the shift checklists, how would we handle schedule changes, etc.

What could possibly go wrong?

My parents shared my dad's medical news with the staff in an employee meeting. Many of our seasoned employees were happy to assist and jump in wherever they could. Their support was certainly a testament to the respect they had for my dad and our family. But a certain portion of the staff members looked as if they were being given an opportunity to coast in his absence. Have you ever heard the phrase "when the cat's away, the mice will play"? As an entrepreneur, become familiar with the sentiment.

Still labeled as the "boss's daughter," I wasn't quite sure I was going to be able to command a team of employees to do as I asked for the next two months. Bear in mind that not only had I never managed anyone before, but on top of that, 75% of the restaurant's employees were 20 years older than me. Having spent time watching my dad, my mom, and Marci manage, I developed a style that I'd like to think took the best management qualities from each of them. My dad and mom played the roles of good cop, bad cop. Marci was like a forensic analyst—nothing got by her, and you didn't dare try. I was the profiler. Blessed with a natural ability to read people and situations, I could anticipate an employee calling out of a shift early or faking an illness. If I was patient and asked enough questions in an affirmative way, I would ultimately get an unprompted apology or confession.

I took a firm approach, but only when I needed to, setting the boundaries while on my watch. I listened to what was being said and made sure to capture all relevant details. I learned that good leaders don't stand around and watch—they lead by example. I worked hand in hand with the team—I bused tables, mopped the floors, peeled potatoes, washed down booths, stacked glasses, and wrapped silverware. I rolled up my sleeves, did the work, and didn't complain.

When my dad recovered fully, I was able to resume my duties as a waitress. However, I was no longer looked at as "the boss's daughter." I had earned the respect of the team and continued to be a sounding board for the employees. Fortunately, our family dinners afforded us the ability to discuss situations as they arose with each other before formally addressing each employee to resolve the situation.

Despite having taken numerous management courses in college and in postgraduate work, I found that I'd spent more time memorizing definitions of managerial buzzwords to ace my exams than learning how to develop a real management style or team management skills. The Avenue provided applicable experiences—a foundation from which I would draw upon over my career. But it wasn't easy.

⌣

"Can you help hostess this morning?" my dad asked on July 4. July 4 is traditionally the biggest day at the Avenue as hundreds of thousands of people visit Gettysburg to see the Civil War reenactments.

"Of course!" The day starts at 6am and doesn't end until 11pm. I was happy to go in and give my dad at least a few hours of calm before we had a line of customers wrapped around the side of the building. I walked through the back door, cheerfully wishing good mornings to the kitchen staff who were preparing for a different kind of battle. As I walked to the front dining room, I could hear loud voices, arguing. The morning shift was standing around the counter arguing over waitress stations. Each waitress is assigned a station or a block of tables, each with the same number of seats. As customers come in, they are rotated in order into those four stations. It's a pretty simple process to follow. It helps us manage the dining room staff and customers, so that we could pace the number of orders being placed in the kitchen.

"Where's your father?" one of the waitresses barked at me.

"He will be in later this morning. Can I help with something?" I asked calmly.

Shirley, one of my favorite people and one of our best employees, explained the situation. That morning, one of the other veteran waitresses decided that she wanted to draw for stations because she was in Station 1. This other waitress was notorious for changing the rules to benefit her—but because of her tenure, no one would stand up to her. I quickly pulled up the station roster to be sure that the stations were properly outlined and then announced to the group that we would be following the original plan.

The veteran waitress immediately threw her notebooks and pounded her fists on the counter. She was yelling. I asked her to calm down and to come back to the office so that we could discuss this rationally.

As we walked back, she then threatened to skip out on her shift if I didn't change her station and give her what she wanted. The entire kitchen staff was silent watching this unfold. I said firmly, "You know the policy. We follow this process, so it is fair to the entire waitstaff. If you choose to walk out on your shift, it is considered an automatic quit per the employee manual. You will no longer be employed at the Avenue."

I remained calm, held my composure. She looked me straight in the eye and said, "Kiss my ass" and then slammed the back door as she left the building.

"Don't let the door hit you on the way out," shouted the head chef. As I turned around, the chef then looked at me and said, "Julie, you're going to be in trouble. Better go call your dad."

I quickly turned and walked into the back office near the kitchen. I called my dad to see if he was on his way in. He said that he was just pulling in. I rushed out to the parking lot, hoping to intercept him before he made it inside the restaurant. This was the busiest week of the year and I had just fired a veteran employee.

As I approached my father, my knees started to shake. I quickly gave him the story from the fighting in the dining room to her parting words to me as she left. He looked at me and said, "Well, did you bring your apron?" We both knew that I always had one in my bag. "Go get ready, you will work her station and shift this morning. Don't worry about it. You did what we should have done a long time ago."

My dad fully supported my decision and did not waver. Most of the staff were relieved that she was gone. She was known for this type of behavior and certainly wasn't one of the top performing employees at the Avenue. When she stopped in a few days later to get her final paycheck, she tried to tell my dad her version of what had happened that morning. She painted my behavior as being aggressive and that I pushed her out for no reason. My dad quickly corrected her. "You and I both know that this is not true. Julie, of all people, is the least aggressive at the restaurant. You knew the policy. You ignored it and left us to cover your shifts during the busiest week of the year. This business is what sustains us in those lean winter months. You made your decision the minute you walked out."

While relieved that I was supported in my decision, I must confess that I didn't walk away feeling great about the experience. That veteran waitress had been with us for a long time. I spent a lot of time working alongside her. She wasn't a bad person. She just wasn't the best fit for this team. This job was still her livelihood and how she supported her family, even though her leaving was the right decision for the business.

Looking back, this experience as an interim manager provided a valuable opportunity to not only learn about managing a team but also how to be a consistent and effective supervisor. I watched how an employee's action or inaction directly affected a team of 25 employees and the bottom line. I became aware of my role in an organization and the value that I brought. I recognized the importance of being dependable and accountable at the Avenue, not as the boss's daughter but as an employee and team member. This set the parameters for my work ethic. I would build on this experience years later as I entered into the professional work environment to start my career.

A few years later, in 2002, I was now a 24-year-old employee in a well-established corporate setting. I reported to the CEO, board of directors, or senior-level management. I remained one or two steps away from the head of the organization. Because of this, I was highly visible to the ultimate decision makers. An avid student, I would listen, learn, and soak up knowledge from keenly watching my managers or my colleagues who were in those coveted roles.

Aside from my parents, my boss at the Institute remains at the top of my list for providing a great example of managerial leadership. His background as a consultant working at one of the top consulting firms in the country likely provided a larger view of how to operate a successful team. I will never forget how he treated me. He was respectful. He acted as if I was an equal. He was patient. He extended opportunities to me to grow in my role and to gain visibility in the Greater Philadelphia business community. He was easy to get along with. He set the expectations high, but not so high that I couldn't reach them. I respected him for knowing that I needed a challenge, even ones that I wasn't confident I could overcome. His management style reminded me of how my dad approached managing his employees.

I am grateful for those most valuable experiences and thankful that my boss at the Institute was a true mentor and leader. He was an exemplary manager.

In contrast, there were other managers whom I worked for who provided me with a different education: an education on the type of leader I didn't want to be. I wasn't afraid of the work or working hard. While disenfranchised by the other managers, I found a way to thrive and survive. I respected that these stake-holders were at or close to the top of the organization but under-stood that just because they were at the top didn't mean that they were effective in managing people.

In my role at the first agency, I managed to hit all the goals and objectives that the CEO had given to me. He told me what publications he wanted to be featured in and noted that no one in the last nine years had even been able to achieve that. I did what I knew best; I got to work and figured out how to get him and the agency recognized in the media. After a few short months, I suc-cessfully garnered him notable speaking opportunities, magazine features on his short list of publications, and nationally published features in publications that he'd not considered. I'll never forget him walking over to my desk and saying "Julie, I don't know how you did it, but this is more than I could have expected. Great job." He later went on to share these same accolades about me at one of our company meetings.

As I prepared for my performance review that year, I was hopeful that these achievements would be considered for a title promotion or possibly even a financial promotion. At that agency, we received performance reviews from management as well as our peers. It was strange to have employees who I'd never worked with directly review my performance. You were scored from one to five—with five being the highest—across different areas. I'll never forget receiving the scores. My peers gave me fives across all areas! But then I was stunned and shocked when the manage-ment for my department scored me at ones in every category. I was speechless!

We had to sit down and review the performance with our direct managers. When I met with my direct manager, he actually gave me lavish praise for the accomplishments that I had made and how I had impressed the CEO by achieving everything that he'd asked for and then some. I was confused as his feedback certainly didn't align with the scores I received on the formal review. I asked him why I would receive such a low score if in fact I was outperforming in my role. My manager was just as shocked as I was when he looked at the review sheet. He had apparently not looked at the formal review in advance of meeting with me to discuss my performance.

I was angry. The fact that my direct manager had not looked at the performance reviews ahead of our meeting showed a complete lack of management skills on his part. And then to see his surprise at the low scores enraged me even more. A few days later, another senior leader pulled me into his office and shared with me where those scores came from. Apparently, the VP above my boss justified my low score by saying that if I could accomplish all of this, then I needed to be motivated to do even more. I was appreciative that the other member of senior leadership pulled me aside to tell me that this comment was totally unwarranted and not a great approach to management.

While I appreciated him for taking the time to find out what had happened with my score, it didn't provide me any solace. Essentially, this VP took it upon himself to score me the lowest possible score as a motivation tactic. Since one was the lowest score possible for each category, I could have shown up every day and done nothing. This was a case of mismanagement and poor communications and a poorly designed approach to management up and down the company hierarchy. I realized I had had enough. As an employee, I could handle constructive feedback or being motivated to do more. However, in this case, this VP intentionally scored me as a one across the board. My performance indicated otherwise and was even recognized and applauded by the owner of the company. I also knew that no matter what I achieved, this senior VP would be in control of my career advancement at the agency. In short, any hopes for my getting ahead would be stymied.

I started looking for new opportunities that night when I got home from work. I was quickly recruited to join another agency for a position that was well suited for my expertise. But as I covered earlier in the book, the new agency proved to have even less capability in terms of management skill. I recall feeling exasperated that with each career move, I'd encounter an environment that was worse than the one before. As an employee, I wasn't looking for praise or accolades. I just wanted to be treated with respect and to be treated fairly. I wanted to have a positive impact on people and the business.

When the time came to start my own business, I thought about the kind of environment I wanted to offer my employees. I made a serious promise to myself that I would never treat my employees in the way that I had been mistreated. I was fortunate to have built an excellent career, but the truth is, I had to overcome a lot of adversity that came from working for executives or managers who were either shortsighted, self-centered, or who just didn't care much about their employees. Those negative experiences have stayed with me and most definitely have had a major influence on how I wanted to run my own business.

As I started to build out my team, I spent some time thinking about my own management philosophy. I didn't formally sit down and type out a dissertation on management, but rather I outlined the key tenets that were important as the business grew. Here are the fundamental management philosophies I strongly believe in:

LEAD BY EXAMPLE

At the Avenue, my dad stressed the importance of understanding all of the job functions at the restaurant. Not only is it important to thoroughly know the overall operations of the business, but it's also vital to understand the responsibilities of each position. Marci and I were asked to work in each position, except for chef, so that we would have an appreciation for each role.

As I started my own business, I also made sure that I understood the responsibilities of each position. I wanted my employees to know that I would not ask them to do work that I could not execute. And when the business requires it, I jump in with the team and complete work, even if it's writing copy for social media or ads. Or if our development team must work through the night preparing for a launch of a website, I stay up with the team, out of solidarity, providing support and encouragement to make it through the long hours.

When at the agency, during a time when I was home suffering through the swine flu, my boss was emailing me incessantly with typos and edits to the master PowerPoint presentation that our team was working on. He sent me no less than 20 emails, demanding a status update or an updated version of the document for review. The changes he requested were so simple that it would have taken him less time to make those changes himself than to actually send 20 emails detailing the requests. It showed me that he was flexing his position and power over me. In this situation, there was really no justification for him to be berating and hounding me, while I was incredibly sick.

As an employee, these experiences have stuck with me. For me, I want to be viewed as a manager who is always prepared to jump in, roll up my sleeves, and get the projects across the finish line without having to harass employees who are out sick.

TREAT PEOPLE WITH RESPECT

It doesn't matter if you are an assistant or a CEO, all people deserve to be treated with respect.

As college students we were told that we had to work hard to earn the respect of our peers or of leadership. As the office environment has shifted in the last 10 years, respect can be earned but the simple practice of treating people with respect goes a long way in building teams.

Follow the Golden Rule in choosing for others what I would choose for myself. As an employee, I knew what it felt like to not be treated as I would treat others, from both a professional and personal perspective. I most certainly didn't want any employee at the firm to ever say that I was not respectful or fair in my treatment of others. Let me give you an example.

One Christmas Eve at 4:30 on a Friday afternoon, I received an unexpected email from a client, who also happened to be the president of a global company. In her note, she ranted and raved about how her reputation had been marred because our team had posted content on a social media platform. The email went to other senior leaders within her organization, my digital team, and our leadership. But the simple truth was that her email was completely emotional, reactive, and inaccurate.

Each year, I give all of our employees off starting December 24 through January 1 so that they can spend much-needed time with their families. All of our clients are notified of this shutdown. If there is an emergency, I am always available. Despite our offices being closed, my team had read the emails. I then quickly replied, clarifying that she and her team had fully approved these posts and that we didn't have any more posts scheduled to go out during the holidays. I would follow up the following Monday. Regardless, she then proceeded to write and send out a rebuttal email to the team with references to bad work ethic and her unhappiness and other items not relevant to my team or their work. It was too late though—my employees had read the emails as they were likely about to celebrate the holidays with their families. I know I was.

I saw this client's actions as another example of poor management. As a leader of a division or a company, sending an angry email at the end of the day on a holiday is a clear indication of what it must be like to work for her. It also showed her inability to be respectful or fair to both teams with her being so completely emotional and irrational in her response. At the end of the day, I just felt bad for her direct subordinate who actually made the mistake as she would have to face her irrational boss at the office on a daily basis. This would have been a perfect opportunity for this boss to have put the Golden Rule into action in her managerial world.

LISTEN FIRST

The main cause for unhappiness in a work environment comes from a lack of understanding or from being misunderstood. In these situations, it's always important to listen first to what is being communicated before reacting. Often, what is being said can be hard to hear. It's human nature to want to feel like you are heard or that you have a voice. As an employer and a manager, I've gained a better understanding of my team and how to motivate a team by trying to be a good and active listener.

This requires complete attention and focus. When employees find the courage to come into my office, whether to discuss a project or a personal issue, I invite them in and close the door so that we can have a private conversation. I mean it when I say that I am accessible and open if there is ever a problem to discuss. I don't have my cell phone in my hand or answer any calls to the office line. I am completely focused on the conversation, ensuring that they walk away from the conversation feeling heard. Even if the conversation is about something trivial to me, it might actually be something really important to that employee. Bottom line? As a boss, work hard at being an active listener.

CONSIDER A DIFFERENT PERSPECTIVE

When you've spent more than 20 years building a career and growing a business, it's easy to lose sight of what it's like for your employees. By understanding their perspective, I am able to identify the best approach to managing each employee.

"Well, I have completed my first year at Junction," an employee noted on her first anniversary. "Only 40 more years to go." I looked up and commented, "Wow! I don't think I've ever looked at work or my career in terms of the number of years I have left to work." She sharply replied, "You wouldn't."

Until this conversation, I had never, not one time, viewed my career or work in terms of years to go until retirement. Yet in this employee's mind, she was putting her time in to get to the end result. I was nearly 20 years older than her, 20 years closer to retirement, and yet I'd never calculated the days, weeks, or years left. I can't tell if I was more shocked at her perspective or her tone when she said, "You wouldn't." It was insightful and certainly telling of how she viewed work. To her this was just a job, a place where she was required to go Monday through Friday and put in her eight hours a day. To me, I looked at her as building the foundation of her career. These are two very different perspectives, with two very different outcomes.

See it from their perspective. I promise that it will prove valuable in understanding what type of employee you will need to manage. It also helps manage your expectations.

OPEN DOOR POLICY

Every day since starting the business, my door has always been open. I tell my employees that if my door is closed, I am either on the phone or in the middle of a project that requires complete focus. I can't count on both hands the number of times that I have closed my door for an entire day.

At the venture capital organization, the doors to the partners' offices were always closed. Walking down the short hallway from my office to my boss's office felt like a mile most days. Oftentimes, I would try to catch him on the way into the office or on his way to a meeting so that I didn't have to knock on his door. It somehow always felt like I was about to get in trouble. My point is, that office never felt open or conducive to interactions or conversations. I made up my mind that I never wanted my own business to ever be like that.

SET BOUNDARIES

As humans, we want to have boundaries or structure placed on us. This is not to say that we love the boundaries that are set for us, but they are needed. It's a delicate balance. In my early career, I found myself in environments that didn't have boundaries set. I was expected to be on call, at all hours of the day, and every day of the week. I was treated as a gal Friday (a term from another generation that referred to administrative assistants). I was also expected to party with my boss and other co-workers on business trips.

As I started my own firm, we had only four people in the office with others working in remote locations. As a small team, it's easy for the lines to be blurred between manager and the employee.

Most entrepreneurs don't develop a management philosophy when they start a business; others will bring years of management training to a new business venture. You can find a number of great books on management if you are at a loss for how to manage and motivate a team. *The One Minute Manager* by Kenneth Blanchard is a favorite. I took his "Gung Ho Training" at an internship before college that I found worthwhile. A few others worth putting on your list, in no particular order:

> » *How to Win Friends and Influence People* by Dale Carnegie
>
> » *The 7 Habits of Highly Effective People* by Stephen Covey
>
> » *Good to Great* by Jim Collins

Surround yourself with knowledge on management whether it's in book form or in peer-to-peer networking groups. Don't be surprised if your management philosophy changes as your business grows and employee expectations demand it.

SET YOUR EXPECTATIONS

There is no question that the business environment has evolved, especially with the impact of COVID-19 on the global employment market and the rise of the millennials and Generation Z. These two generations enter the work environment with a set of unique expectations that is unlike generations before. When I entered the workplace, I was prepared to put in the work and do what was required and more to make an impact on each environment that I went into. I arrived at work early, stayed late, and extended myself if others needed my assistance, even if the tasks fell outside of my immediate responsibility. I was diligent in my efforts and respectful in my interactions with all levels of the organization, always careful to not overstep my position. I was happy to receive a five-dollar parking voucher, attend a free work dinner, or receive a restaurant gift card at the holidays. I didn't expect anything but appreciated whatever I did receive. As an entrepreneur, I was excited at building a team of high performers who resembled myself when I entered the workforce. Finding these types of employees is like hunting for a needle in a digital haystack. Yet, I've been encouraged by a stable of core employees who have stuck with the business for several years. The good experiences far outweigh the negative experiences, but both have provided a training ground for the development of my management approach and leadership skills.

"We are out of Coke, did you order more?" an employee asked at the entrance to my office. I looked up at her and said, "If there isn't any in the supply closet or the refrigerator, then we must not have any. I will order more with the next office order." I returned to what I was working on, not paying too much attention to the conversation. Again, the following day, that same employee asked on her way to the kitchen if I had a chance to pick up Coke for her. I reminded her that I would order it with our next office order in four days as it was nearly the end of the month.

In our project management system, we have a project for the main office. I encourage employees to put in their requests for the types of snacks or drinks that they like. The order is placed at the beginning of each month. We order enough to keep the team snacking. If for some reason the snacks/specialty drinks run out before the end of the month, then we are out until the next office order. We aren't a convenience store, but we are in an office park that has four or five restaurants, a specialty grocer, a gas station and convenience store, and a Starbucks, all within 200 yards or so of the front of our office building. Yes, they are all that close.

The next day, as a few of us prepared to order lunch on Door-Dash, that same employee looked over at me and said, "Can you order a Coke with your order since we are out in the office? I don't want to have to go buy one." I pursed my lips, smiled, and walked back into my office. I ordered her a Coke with my order. I walked into her office, asked her if she needed me to open it, and then asked if she was happy. She looked at me a little bewildered.

"I'm fine. It's fine. It's all going to be fine."

Her relentless expectation was just one example of the ever-present "entitlement" behavior from her. I was disappointed in my own behavior—as I surely wasn't leading by example when I asked her if I could open it for her. While I expect that employees like the perks of free snacks, the behavior was not just entitled but disrespectful. She was completely capable of bringing her own Coke to work or walking to grab one at lunch. Instead, she spent three days asking me, the CEO of the company, where the Coke was, much like a child nagging a parent for a snack.

Over the course of a year and a half, I shrugged off what I considered to be childish behavior or disrespectful comments that she would say from time to time. She would often complain to me that her friend made more money, a lot more, than she did. She even complained just before we gave her a 10% raise after only six months with the company. She went on to receive a $2,000 bonus at the holiday and a 10% raise at her annual review two months later. At which point, she expressed rudely that it wasn't enough and that she expected more.

My management experience had taught me that you can't manage this behavior out of an employee. She was a good employee, but with a bad attitude and unrealistic expectations. She carried entitlement around the office, in her interactions with me and other team members. Previous behavior is always indicative of future behavior. I didn't have the time or the desire to try and change her mind in this case. She decided to resign not long after.

As a business owner, it's always disappointing when someone decides to leave the company. I believe in the environment that I've created. In her case, she came to our firm right out of college. From her first day forward, she'd make comments on what she didn't like, almost as if she'd settled for the position. It's still disappointing when I think back on her time with the company. She had potential but her attitude would limit her, not just at my company but in her future endeavors. In the end, she didn't have other experiences to compare this to. In her mind, the grass would always be greener on the other side of the fence. So, this was her opportunity to find out.

And following her exit, I re-established my own boundaries with new employees as to what should be expected. As a leader, it's my job to set the expectation. I forget sometimes that while I can set expectations for myself, in many cases, I must set different expectations for my employees. More importantly, it's critical that our own expectations are aligned.

I always tell people that the hardest part of owning a business is the people. It's hard to find great people, to keep those people, and to avoid getting dismayed by the wrong people. I can tell you that I have spent more time thinking about the "Coke" situation—analyzing what I could have done better to improve the outcome.

You will never be the perfect manager or create a utopian work environment. Accept this first. Then, learn from each experience. Let them guide future decisions as it relates to management and building a team.

IMPORTANT DETAILS

»   Always lead by example.

»   Treat everyone with respect and by how you would expect to be treated.

»   Set clear and consistent boundaries.

CHAPTER SIX

⌒

THE ART OF COMMUNICATION

Communication is the fundamental skill required to survive and to thrive in business. As a young child, I aspired to be Barbara Walters or Tom Brokaw. I listened intently to how they spoke and the words that they used to tell a story. To say I was passionate about communication is an understatement. I have always been a purveyor of the written and spoken word. To me, words are an opportunity to create real impact.

The late MIT professor Patrick Winston was an avid lecturer to students and entrepreneurs on the importance of communication. In his words, "Your success in life will be determined largely by your ability to speak, your ability to write, and the quality of your ideas, in that order." He especially thought this relevant for entrepreneurs.

Growing up in the 80s and 90s, in a small town, all forms of communication were mostly in person with an occasional phone call or mailed letter. Working as a waitress as a teenager provided an excellent opportunity for me to speak with different people from all corners of the globe. With each conversation, I learned techniques for starting and growing a conversation. I even learned techniques for avoiding sensitive topics or exiting a conversation delicately. Many of those conversations I would detail in my journals, writing about how those individuals and words affected my life, whether positively or negatively. These experiences were invaluable when I moved to Paris and had to learn how to communicate confidently in a new language. Today, my ability to speak and communicate with other people, whether in business or in life, is one of my greatest gifts. A gift that has allowed me to progress in my career.

"Do you have the script and logistics prepared?" my boss asked. "We need to get this solidified and distributed to everyone who is speaking at the event. For each person, highlight the times and lines that they need to pay attention to."

At the Institute, we hosted many events throughout the year, which included folks from the venture communities in Greater Philadelphia. To ensure that the event ran smoothly from the welcome to the closing remarks, we prepared a script and logistics that detailed the timeline and what was to be spoken at the podium. An example of this document started with:

5:35 Announcement to Be Seated

5:40 Welcome Remarks

(INSERT NAME) Welcome colleagues and partners to the INSERT EVENT NAME hosted by INSERT COMPANY NAME. We are gathered this evening to honor entrepreneurs who are building new businesses in our communities...

7:45 Closing Remarks

8:00 Event Concludes

These scripts were tedious to prepare. We were not just outlining the timeline but also creating the actual content for each participant. It was as though we were preparing a script for a movie, although without information on lighting and scenery. For the first year and a half, I was responsible for creating these scripts. I would manage the master document and follow along as the event progressed, much like a director on a set. There is no greater feeling of satisfaction watching this event play out just as you've written it.

I do remember thinking this was a lot of effort for what felt like a simple event, until the day came when my boss was sick and unable to attend the event. I had received notice just 30 minutes before the event that he would not be able to be there and that I was to carry on in his place.

"Follow the script and you will be fine. Be confident. Speak slowly. Look at the audience. I will check in with you after the event," he coached via email as reality started to hit. I was now going to be the main emcee for an event in front of 50 to 100 people. I was paralyzed at the thought of standing in front of this crowd. With no time to prepare, I took out a highlighter and quickly noted my sections to read from the podium.

As the event started, I was pleasantly surprised. In the process of writing, editing, and rewriting this script, I had managed to memorize the words. As a result, I was able to focus more on my voice and presence. From at first being completed terrified, I received applause and even a few compliments on how well I did under the circumstances. Make no mistake, this was not a stroke of good luck. This was a result of being completely and totally prepared from the first line to my closing statement. I stuck to the script.

The opportunities for me to speak in front of groups of entrepreneurs, business leaders, and colleagues would continue. What started with a room of 50 people would slowly turn into groups of 400 or more attendees in my two and a half years at the Institute.

When I was then recruited by the venture capital organization, the managing partner told me that he was always so impressed with how well I spoke and carried myself in these crowds. I had found my voice and learned how to project confidence. And as I would learn, those folks at my events were listening.

⌁

"Daymond John arrives in 20 minutes. I will sit at the table with him and his team. You will need to run the show. Don't screw it up. Everyone will be watching," said the managing partner, minutes before our venture event started.

It was 2005. This venture event would bring together 400 private equity investors, venture capitalists, angel investors, institutional investors, and selected entrepreneurs from New England to North Carolina. Daymond John, founder of FUBU, graciously agreed to be our keynote speaker. At the time, he was looking to network with investors and source investment opportunities to grow his portfolio, long before he would be on *Shark Tank*.

In addition to managing the entire event with my staff, I was also responsible for being the master of ceremonies for the breakfast keynote address, the lunch keynote address, and the closing remarks. I was 26, young, blond, and female, in a room full of accomplished and successful leaders, all of them more than 20 years my senior.

"I'm fine. It's fine. It will all be fine."

It was standing room only in the main ballroom, in anticipation of Daymond John's keynote address. Daymond was sitting with his team in the front row, center table. I made the mistake of looking out across the room only to discover 800 eyes staring right in my direction. I was so nervous, I was shaking. I wanted to hide. I took to the stage, armed with my script and logistics. I took a deep breath. I adjusted the microphone. I looked at the crowd, lifted my head, smiled, and began to speak.

I hit every cue, followed the script, and delivered what I considered to be one of my best performances. Throughout the day, many attendees approached me to congratulate me on a job well done. They commented on how eloquent and engaging I was. It made me feel good.

After the event, I was proud of the success we had achieved. I was also proud of how far I had come from waitressing at my parents' restaurant to speaking to a packed house full of really important people. It was a career high, a direct result of my total preparation.

The preparation started months before the event. I had worked through at least six versions of this script before I had submitted it for approval. I was editing my remarks just hours before the event that morning. I had practiced the speech at least 50 times in the weeks leading up to the event. I practiced in my car during my 45-minute commute back and forth to the office.

If I missed a line or messed up, I would go back to the beginning and start again. I'd run lines by my dad and my mom. My roommate would catch me reciting the speech while I was making dinner or cleaning the house. In short, I was prepared.

We often think that great speakers are just born with the ability to speak in front of large crowds or carry on a conversation that everyone is engaged in. To be great at speaking, you must put in the work. And the work starts long before you step behind the podium. It takes real practice, focus, and a commitment to communicating well.

Not all entrepreneurs start a business with these kinds of speaking experiences. Most will not. But if you can't communicate well, it can be the difference between success or failure.

In 2000, I entered the workforce before Gmail existed, in work environments that relied on in-person or inter-office memos. Yes, those old yellow inter-office envelopes with printed notes. We would type up our messages, proofread, print, and then secure them via an inter-office envelope. We would then put the date, time, destination, and person for which this message was for. Our inter-office mail courier would come by two times per day to pick up the envelopes and distribute accordingly. Receiving a response could take several business days, despite being located less than 200 yards from the person we were trying to reach. And if there was a mistake in the communication, the process would start all over again.

During my initial 90-day probationary period, my boss would require that any communication that I was to send from our office was to be properly proofread. I was expected to print each email, press release, event flyer, or article, and then pop into his office for the "red pen" reviews. I would sit across from him at a little round table in his office. He would read through each document and make notes and edits in red pen. We would discuss the edits ad nauseum. I would then retreat to my desk, make the assigned edits, and return once again for the next round of edits. The pages were a blood bath of red ink.

I dreaded those meetings. Feeling indignant, I would complain to co-workers at how ridiculous this process was. I worked for a PR agency for the top fashion photographers, speaking only in French, and yet I couldn't seem to escape death by red pen on a simple note to an internal stakeholder or external partner?

And while it pained me to admit it then, my boss knew what he was doing. He didn't just mark the mistakes. He explained why he made those edits. He provided perspective on how a person would receive the message and how it could be misinterpreted. I opened my mind and my ears. Within a couple of months, we didn't have any red pen reviews anymore and he signed off quickly on my notes.

Looking back, this process made me a better communicator. I was diligent and deliberate in all of my communications, whether a printed document or in a face-to-face meeting. But my boss showed me how critically important it was to be precise, succinct, and right to the point in my memos. Communicating well is the lifeblood of any business and cannot be taken for granted.

As technology progressed, email and digital tools took over how we communicated internally and with external audiences. For many of you, Communications is a basic-level course you took in college to fulfill the prerequisite. For others, you will have grown up with technology, with 140-character messages, and an endless array of emojis. Regardless of your age or experience, mastering the art of communications is critical to being successful. Communications will be at the core of every interaction with internal and external audiences and often starts with what is considered a simple form of communication. Email.

"Julie, sorry to have to call you this morning about this. One of our account managers brought a situation to my attention today regarding an email from your team," explained our main stakeholder at Yahoo!. "She's upset with the communication that has been going back and forth. She mentioned that the email is short and didn't even include a salutation, which she takes great offense to."

I could feel the color drain from my face as she spoke. I was a little shocked that this even warranted a direct phone call yet I was embarrassed that an email salutation was the reason for this discussion. We'd successfully delivered over 600 creative assets in one calendar year, flawlessly. Our fine record had now been blemished due to an email salutation? I immediately apologized and promised that I would address this immediately with the team. Moving forward, all future emails would always include a name and a salutation. If I am honest, she was right. Even today, when I receive an email that doesn't start with "hi," "hello," or my first name, I immediately cringe. If I were to call an individual on the phone, I always start with "Hi, this is Julie Gareleck from Junction." Can you imagine if I just launched right into the conversation? No.

This occurred just two years into the business. It was an experience that I never wanted to have with any other client. As someone who takes great pride in how she communicates, I felt like we had failed at one of the most basic tasks at the company. As a new leader, mindful of imposing too many rules on my employees, I knew it would be a delicate topic to discuss, unless it was considered a company policy. So, as a company, we started a Main Resource Document that has since grown to more than 60 pages. What started as guidelines to document process and procedure has turned into a manual for how we communicate internally and externally at Junction. I felt pride when one of our rock star employees referred to it as the "Junction Bible," providing quick and important answers to just about any question.

For example, at my firm, we define the font, font color, and font size for all communications or deliverables. We have developed specific guidelines on how to communicate with our clients from a simple introductory call to the delivery of a comprehensive marketing strategy. We do this so that our clients and colleagues receive consistent communications, whether it's from a project manager with two years of experience or a senior leader with more than 20 years of experience. You would not be shocked to know that we also have consistent salutations too. Here's a sample of what you'd find in our document:

Communication Guidelines *(Also refer to the Sample Project Emails section of this document)*

- » Email Subjects: Capitalize the subject line as you would a title, beginning everything except minor words with capital letters

- » Salutation and Sign-Off: Use an acceptable salutation with the client's first name. Likewise, use an acceptable sign-off with your first name.

  - Acceptable Salutations: Hi [First Name], Hello [First Name], Good Morning [First Name] Good Afternoon [First Name]

  - Acceptable Sign-offs: Sincerely, Thanks, Best Regards (Note that we prefer Sincerely)

  - Be consistent in your usage

  - For reference, Julie begins all of her emails to clients with "Hi [Client first name]," and ends with "Sincerely, Julie"

- » Font Requirements: As an agency, we use Calibri 11pt for body font, and Calibri 14 for Title font. Always be sure to check the fonts in email before sending to client. Pasting into and out of Basecamp can affect formatting, especially for bullet points.

- » Timing Requirement: Absolutely no emails or other communication with clients outside of normal business hours (8am to 6pm) unless there is a critical exception!

» Deliverables Goal: Our goal is to send client deliverables no later than 3pm so that we are not scrambling to deliver by close of business.

» Responsiveness: On average, the goal is to respond to all client emails within 1-4 business hours. There are certainly exceptions; but this is the average expected response time.

» Tone: Junction is friendly but professional.

» Be concise but specific. Provide context of what it is you are sending to the client, and any items you need from them with the dates you expect to receive them.

» Recap meeting action items

» Reiterate next steps in the process

» Always include your full contact information in the footer of the email

» Spell-check always

No texting. As an agency, we do not text clients. The only possible exception to this would be if you are running early/late for a meeting, but even in this case, a phone call would be the preferred method of communication. Texting is too informal, can provide inconsistent communication, and the rest of the team is also left out of the communication.

⌒

When I started this agency, I had no idea how important this Resource Document would become. We have painstakingly documented communication templates for nearly every project stage or type of project that comes in and out of our agency. The email templates are fully outlined for all employees to view and use as needed in their current job role. Here is an example:

Follow Up to Introductory Email 2 (Requesting Kick-Off Availability)

Email Subject: [Respond to Initial Thread]

Hi [Client Name],

I look forward to working with you on this project!

As Julie noted in her email, we would like to schedule a kick-off call with you to review the project requirements and align expectations. We will schedule the call for 1 hour [or make this 30 minutes if we don't have much to go over or it's a smaller project] and include key team members who will be working on the project.

Our team is available for the kick-off call on [Dates] between [Times] ET. Please provide alternate times if these days/times do not work. Once confirmed, I will follow up with a Zoom invitation for the call.

I look forward to your response!

Sincerely,
[Your Name]

For many of our employees, it's shocking the level of detail we go to. As part of the initial onboarding process, Susan, our Director of Account, spends the first two training sessions going over this document and our project management system. Employees are to spend additional time reading and becoming familiar with the information in this document. We encourage our team to first reference this document before asking management the question. Nine times out of ten, the answer is available within this document. We require employees to submit email drafts for review by the Director of Account during a probationary period. It's so important to us that we all communicate in the right format and tone and with the right context. It might seem like a simple email, but it serves as the core way that we communicate with our clients.

Susan and I often question whether we've provided too much information to our employees. We worry that we take all the thinking out of the process. We always arrive at the same conclusion. Those employees who embrace this tool in their positions succeed at our firm. Those that remain indignant with this process don't succeed.

I take great pride in the fact that we've not had a client complain about how we communicate. An early lesson in business inspired a commitment to communicating the right way. Don't discount the unexpected value that a proper communications strategy will be for your business. Let me explain what I mean from the email I received one day from a client:

"I would have expected, you understand our concern and offer to make any changes in order to exceed our expectations. I own three highly reputable businesses and employ over 200 people. This is an insult to my intelligence. I will patiently wait until Monday, May 16th for a full refund otherwise, I will dispute the charge with my credit card company and have our attorney get involved in this case. I will also file a complaint with BBB and share our experience with other platforms including, clutch, semrush, agencyspotter, upcity, google, yelp etc..."

A gut punch on a Wednesday morning. We had worked with this client for over three months on a small website project. We had delivered a website test link for the client's review earlier that week, along with a reference to the approved documentation from the earlier phases in the project. We had communicated that several of his requests fell outside of the original scope of the project. We had already allocated over 35 hours of additional work as an investment in the relationship. We asked for a meeting to review this test link and to review his additional requests so that our team could effectively estimate the level of effort to complete the work.

You just read his response above.

Until this angry exchange, all communications between our team and his team, via email and over the phone, had been pleasant. In fact, we even remarked internally on how refreshing this client was to deal with. I was shocked by his reaction, but even more so disappointed in how he chose to communicate.

Sadly, this client lobbed a threat and a promise to damage our reputation. He also chose to put it in writing and copy my entire team and his corporate counsel. Within a few hours, our team was able to organize all the documentation, approved deliverables, and email correspondence clarifying the scope and reiterating expectation from our first email with this client to this last exchange.

I responded to the client directly, stating that I take threats to my business very seriously and that his threat was motivated by his desire to simply get additional work at no cost. I included the documentation as evidence for his counsel should he decide to pursue this path. In the end, we delivered the final files to the client without further incident. He didn't dispute the charges and even ended up taking the final website files for his use. He did, however, note that since we weren't willing to finish the job at no cost, he would have to hire another firm to complete the work.

Confident in our documentation, process, and communication, I was not worried about any potential legal exposure. For my team, it was abundantly clear why Susan and I go to such lengths with our communications and process. This example proved our "why." It also served as a solid lesson to our team. In this situation my client provided an example of how not to communicate. Is this how he communicated with his employees, his clients, and his other partners? We were likely not the first firm to be on the receiving end of one of his emails. We would likely not be the last.

In hindsight, I do believe that if we were able to schedule a meeting to discuss all of this with the client, I could have steered us in a productive conversation on how to best move forward. In difficult situations, it's easy to hide behind email.

As you start a business or progress in your career, always be mindful of how impactful words in an email can be.

⌒つ

Dale Carnegie, author of the classic bestseller *How to Make Friends and Influence People*, wrote that "**90 percent** of all management problems are caused by miscommunication." The percentage is likely just as high with peer-to-peer or client communication. Miscommunication is directly linked to lost time, money, and sentiment, which will limit opportunities for your company's success. By focusing on the fundamentals of great communication first, you are preparing yourself for valuable interactions that could lead to business growth.

Even with more than 20 years of experience, I still prepare a script for meetings and sales pitches. I practice aloud when I am getting ready in the morning or driving to work. I memorize the details. I concentrate on my tone. I take my time. Yes, I still get nervous, but I know at the core, I am prepared. And believe it or not, when tasked to assist my team if my number two is out of the office, I still open the Resource Document first. I use it as a guide to review our team's communications. I also use the templates that we've created to ensure that the communication is seamless. While I haven't memorized every single page, I smile every time I find answers to my questions in the document. Bottom line? Don't get lost in 140 characters. Always use a salutation. And if nothing else, learn from my early hard-earned lessons. Success is in the details.

IMPORTANT DETAILS

» Your success in business relies on your ability to speak clearly and to write well.

» Develop guidelines for how you would like your employees to communicate to clients and colleagues. Be specific.

» Remember: 90% of all management issues stem from miscommunication.

CHAPTER SEVEN

IT'S IN THE DETAILS

As I walk through the back door, I can hear the clatter of dishes, the din of silverware being sorted by the dishwasher, and the swish of the swinging door as servers rush in and out to grab their orders. I take a deep breath as I walk into the front dining room. Every one of the 110 seats are full and there is a line 20 deep wrapped outside around the front of the restaurant. I quickly tie my apron, grab my notepad and pen. I check in with the host to see which table is first. As I walk the last few steps to my table, I take a deep breath, look up, and smile.

"Good morning, my name is Julie! I will be your server today. May I start you off with something to drink?"

"We are ready to order," the customer responds curtly.

"Absolutely, I am ready for your order when you are!" I respond.

While the young, immature side of me wanted nothing more than to roll my eyes as I walked away from the table, I learned from waiting on thousands of people that you won't always be met with a smile and a hello. When I first started waiting tables, I would let disgruntled customers get under my skin. Over time though, rather than getting upset, I would adapt my approach to customers based on how I read them as I said hello.

Effectively, I was reading the psychology of the customers. As you build a business, being able to read a room, colleagues, or clients is just as important as building a solid foundation in communication. My experience over nearly a decade of waiting on customers from all over the world provided great insight into honing my ability to read people and situations. I am not suggesting that you need to get a degree in psychology, but rather learn more about the techniques designed to help you better understand your employees, clients, and colleagues.

BODY LANGUAGE

Believe it or not, the actual words that we use represent only a small percentage of how we communicate with each other. Body language and the tone of your voice represent more than 80% of how we communicate. As a waitress, in the final steps toward their table, I learned to look at the customers' appearance, how they carried themselves, and what expressions I could see on their faces.

INTUITION

Intuition has served me well in my personal and professional life. I've learned from experience to always trust my "gut." In most cases, it's really a nonverbal feeling I feel when I meet someone for the first time or start a dialogue. In other situations, it's an immediate visceral reaction that signals whether I can trust this person. In any situation, you *must* pay attention to the details. While not a perfect science, intuition is instinctive. Don't ignore it.

ENERGY

Energy is an expression of our emotions. Like intuition, you are essentially reading the vibes that a person is giving off. I find that reading a person's energy is more complex than feeling an initial gut reaction. I break it down into three parts. The first thing I notice about a person is their presence. Are they upbeat or are they reserved? Do they carry themselves with confidence? Do they look like they are hiding something? You can learn even more by looking a person in the eye or when you extend your hand for a handshake.

Just an hour before the restaurant closed, a family of six was seated in my station in the back dining room. As I approached the table, I was struck by a feeling that unsettled me. The woman, who I assumed was the mother, placed an order for six milkshakes, six drinks, and six waters for the table. When I returned with the drink order, she proceeded to order four appetizers, two bowls of soup, four burgers with fries for her children, a porterhouse steak for her husband, and for her baked flounder stuffed with crabmeat (coincidently this was the most expensive entrée on our menu). She was rough when she spoke and had a loud voice that carried across the dining room. The kids were climbing all over the booths. The husband sat with his head down, hands in his lap, and did not look up at me once. Something just felt off with this family, but I couldn't pinpoint why.

As I walked into the kitchen with the order, the cooks asked how many people were really at the table. The order was enough food to feed ten people. They were not wrong. When I delivered the appetizers and soups, I just couldn't help but wonder where this family was from and why I was so bothered by them. I later delivered the entrées without incident. Five minutes later, I checked on the family to see how they were enjoying the meal. The woman immediately started yelling at me, loud enough for the dining room to hear.

She claimed that a cook left a hair in her flounder. She lifted it up and I could see that it was a bleached hair with black roots, an exact match for the hair on her head. It was then that I realized she was trying to get away with a free meal. Knowing that our chefs wore hairnets, and both happened to have shaved jet-black hair, I took the dinner back, which, by the way, she had nearly finished eating. I offered to make her another entrée. She claimed that she was too disgusted to eat and demanded that she not be charged for the meal.

Our policy at the restaurant was to offer an alternate meal if a customer was unhappy. However, we were trained to look for customers who were attempting to get a free meal. Judging from the completely empty plates on the table, I assumed she was looking for a free meal for the most expensive item on their ticket.

"I will check with the manager to see what we can do," I said as I walked back to tally the bill. The kids skipped out of the restaurant, running around outside while she and her husband waited at the table. I dropped the bill at the table and told her that we had removed the cost of the baked flounder. She sneered at me and said a few choice words about the entire experience being horrible. The husband politely asked where the men's room was and took the bill from the table. The woman stood up and huffed out.

I cleared a few dishes and walked them back into the kitchen. Still feeling unsettled, I asked my mom, who was managing the register that night, if the man had given her any trouble when paying the bill. She looked at me and said, "I don't have the bill, which table are you talking about? He never stopped by."

Alarmed, I quickly walked back to the bathrooms, only to find both empty. He had left without paying. I immediately had my mom call the police so that we could report the theft of service for the nearly $200 bill.

"The wife was wearing a white smocked dress, with at least 20 different gold bracelets on each arm. She had bleached hair with black roots showing through. Her husband was wearing a purple Puma soccer jersey, light blue jean shorts, and Adidas sneakers. They had four children with them, all seemed to be under the age of 13, one girl and three boys. They were all dressed in clothes that were tattered and they all looked as if they had not showered."

The police officer looked up from his notepad and asked, "What made you think to memorize what this family looked like?"

"Well, I just had a gut feeling when I walked up to the table that something didn't seem right. There was just a feeling I could not shake."

"Thank you for this description. It's a busy night here in town. We will put out an alert to patrol the area. We will follow up if we find the family," the officer said to me and my parents as he walked out of the restaurant.

My dad received a call the next morning at eight o'clock from the police department. He explained that they were able to locate this woman and her family from the description I provided. As it turned out, the woman had outstanding warrants for her arrest in multiple states for identify theft, credit card fraud, jewelry theft, and several petty crime offenses. Her husband also had outstanding warrants, but they were unable to locate him that evening.

My dad was given the option of pressing charges or allowing her to settle her bill. He opted for her to come settle her bill. The same officer brought her in to pay the bill.

"Your detailed description of this woman and her family was spot-on," he chuckled when he saw me standing behind the counter. "You sure you don't want my job?"

Nearly 20 years later, I can still remember what the family looked like, what they were wearing, and what they ordered. My intuition was not wrong.

I had the benefit of waiting on thousands of individuals before I started my own chosen career. It was the best psychology course I could ever take. It would prove to be even more valuable than a $200 dinner.

ALWAYS TRUST YOUR GUT INSTINCT

It was 2006. I had recently moved to Atlanta, from Philadelphia, to live closer to Steve, my boyfriend. Since Steve left Wall Street, he has been building his companies and growing entrepreneurial ventures. One of his businesses was in the process of acquiring a software company. Steve mentioned that we were going to have a barbeque with a few of his colleagues and wanted to introduce me to the owner of the company his firm was acquiring.

"This is my girlfriend, Julie," introduced Steve.

I looked the CEO in the eye, smiled, and I extended my hand. "It's a pleasure to meet you. Steve has said so many great things about you," I said.

He grabbed my hand in an awkward handshake. "Nice to meet you. So, what do you do all day while Steve is at work, play tennis?" he asked.

Offended at the implication, I quickly summarized my background in Philadelphia and explained that I was working as a strategist. Within seconds, his eyes lowered, and his head dropped. He said, "Oh, so you are a smart one." Just as awkward as the handshake, he darted across the room to fill up his drink. Those would be the only words I would speak to him that night. There was something about him I didn't trust, and it made me almost sick to my stomach.

Later than evening, Steve and I were standing in the kitchen talking after the barbeque. "So, is this deal with the CEO finalized or are you still doing due diligence?" I asked.

"The paperwork has been signed. Why would you ask a question like that?" Steve said.

"I don't get a good vibe from him. There is something that isn't right," I responded.

"What? You barely talked to him," Steve said.

"I don't know, he wouldn't look me in the eye when he spoke to me and he basically walked away from the conversation when he learned what my background was. Being in the same room with him made me nervous."

"Julie, that is ridiculous. You don't know him. We've done our due diligence. And you don't really understand the business," Steve responded, seeming annoyed with the entire conversation.

He was right. I didn't know this man. I didn't know his business. But I had a visceral reaction to meeting him and just felt like he was hiding something. My gut is never wrong? Out of respect for Steve, I didn't bring it up again. That is, of course, until we had learned that this man single-handedly moved millions of dollars of business to a competitor while acting as the CEO of Steve's company. Not only did this cost millions of dollars in loss to his company, but it also cost many employees their jobs, and this man tried to ruin Steve's reputation in the industry. He even managed to rope in the VP of Sales into his web of deceit.

It took seven years and over a million dollars to fight this man in court. While Steve never recovered the lost revenue, we were successful in getting the court to find him guilty on several charges. In the process, Steve was able to repair the reputational harm that came of this man's deceit and lies.

My gut was in fact not wrong. Steve and I both recall that conversation in the kitchen that night and Steve acknowledges that he should have paid more attention or dug a little deeper into this man's background. And since that time, Steve continues to have me meet with executives he is interested in bringing into his businesses and to get my opinion. My intuition is sharp, and I've gotten good at reading people, even from just a casual conversation over appetizers. Steve has learned to appreciate this ability, whether he likes what my gut has to say or doesn't agree with my assessment of a handshake.

LEARN HOW TO "READ" YOUR CLIENTS

Not only do I apply these same principles in my own business, but these same principles are also critical to the development of an effective marketing strategy. Junction Creative arms clients with knowledge related to the wants, needs, and motivations of customers. If we understand the unique psychology of each customer and how they consume information, we speak directly to them, whether on social media, print, or other channels and engage them in a conversation. My team has heard me talk at great length about the importance of reading our clients, about listening to how they speak or what they say, so that we can better understand their perspectives. Not only does it provide insights into how the partnership will develop, but it enables us to adapt our methods to speak with them in a way that they want to receive the information.

Just before COVID-19 shut down the world, I scheduled a tour of the Northeast to meet with our clients and prospective clients. Susan, a project manager, and I visited three cities in three days. We started the trip in Wilmington, Delaware, then stopped in Philadelphia for dinner and a meeting, before driving to Harrisburg for strategy meetings. In preparation for the meetings, I pulled together research and background information on the company and the people that we would be meeting. I circulated it to the team for review in advance of the trip. We had not met many of these clients in person yet.

Our first meeting was with a financial services firm in Wilmington, Delaware. The client team was incredibly professional and definitely had more of a conservative setting. We methodically moved through our agenda and outline, making sure to stay on time and task. As it was a discovery meeting, we asked a lot of foundational questions and provided recommendations for how to best accomplish the goals they were looking to attain. We let the client do most of the talking. When I started to notice their body language shift, likely because we were all starving, we wrapped up our session with a quick discussion of next steps. A great dialogue and productive conversation all around.

The next morning, we were to meet with a large commercial developer in Philadelphia. This firm had experienced explosive growth and needed a custom solution to manage each one of their developments. The individuals who we were meeting with were part of the veteran team, all having worked at this firm for many years. We arrived five minutes early to the meeting and greeted the receptionist as we entered the building.

We were ushered quickly to a conference room. We were told the team would be in shortly. Within minutes, six people came into the room and took their seats. I started with my usual pleasantries but was met with cold stares and no response. Awkward doesn't aptly describe the mood in the room. As if by second nature, I quickly pivoted and launched directly into the purpose for the meeting. The pace was fast. The tone was one of serious direction. It was less of a conversation and more of a Q&A session, which lasted less than 30 minutes. The leader of the client team then said, "Well, what are your recommendations?" I explained that in order to aptly assess the platforms, we would need a few days to complete additional research.

"You have until Friday." With that, we stood up, gathered our things quickly, and hurried out of the building. We didn't speak to each other until we were a block away and inside of our car.

As I settled into the front passenger seat, I nervously laughed and said, "Well, how do we think the meeting went? Was I able to recover?"

Despite being extremely prepared for the meeting, the reaction of this client team was unlike any I had experienced in the recent years. In this case, we were met with cold, blank stares and folded arms. All of the years of practice certainly helped as I rebounded after a failed introduction and hello.

"It's fascinating how you run these meetings. It's interesting to watch you match the tone and the speed of the people we are meeting with," the project manager commented.

"What? Do I really?" I asked.

"Yes, you just did it in that meeting. When you walked in and said 'Good morning, how are you today?' we were met with blank stares. It was the most uncomfortable silence. And then you just started talking directly and got down to business, no pleasantries. It was completely different than our meetings yesterday."

"I don't realize that I am doing that," I commented. "I should know from having started my career in Philadelphia. People talk fast and more directly. After the silent pause, it's almost like I switched over to Philadelphia Julie. It also dawned on me that the Eagles had lost a home game last night, and they were all likely up late watching the game. Having a meeting with our team at eight in the morning was the last place they wanted to be," I chuckled.

Being able to effectively read people or a read a room is a very important skill. Conducting research and putting together background notes is important, but the truth is, it doesn't fully prepare you for how to operate or run a meeting when it starts. Much like my experiences at the restaurant, when I take the last few steps before entering a sales meeting or a client location, I focus intently on the environment, the people, body language, tone, and facial expressions. As if by second nature, I adjust my approach to align with the energy in the room.

In a virtual or hybrid environment, I am not always able to read the room, but the principles still apply to virtual interactions. I still adapt my approach even after all these years of owning my own firm. After this experience in Philadelphia, I became even more aware of how my own body language and tone affects my clients, which is not always to my benefit in some cases.

"Good afternoon, Junction Creative, this is Julie speaking!" I chime as I pick up the office line.

"Julie, it's me," a client stated directly.

"Hi! How are you doing on this fine Wednesday?" I replied.

"Geez, Julie. Every time I call you, you are just so pessimistic and low energy," he said sarcastically.

"Yes, I apologize. I'll try to be less enthusiastic for you," I chuckled.

A glass "always full" kind of individual, I realize that in some cases my optimistic personality can be a little much for some of my clients. In my experience working with this client, I realized that his general affect was a glass "almost empty" approach to most anything we had discussed. Rarely was there a silver lining to the rain clouds swirling above him. He was direct when he spoke, raised his voice if he thought we didn't hear him, and acted as though we were a persistent thorn in his side. While we always maintain the highest level of professionalism, it was hard to hear that I was like a cheerleader at a funeral.

As with any interaction you have with a colleague or client, it's critical to not just pay attention to the body language and the tone. In this case, I knew if this relationship was going to be successful, I needed to bring down my sentiment to align with how he liked to be communicated with. You have to be sensitive to how others want to receive messaging.

Knowing this, I adjusted my approach. When I caught his name on caller ID, I said, "Hey Tom," in a lower, less enthusiastic tone, instead of my normal greeting. He would launch into the reason for the call. I'd listen and not speak until I was sure that he was finished. Rather than answer all his questions, I would tell him that I would check with the team and get a response back to him as soon as possible. Sometimes, I'd get a "thanks" before he hung up the phone. He wasn't a bad client. He just communicated differently. And at the end of the project, he provided praise to the team for a job well done and looked forward to working with us again. In the future when I see his name on caller ID, I will know to try and temper my enthusiasm when I answer his calls!

As you start hiring employees and adding clients, remember these simple techniques. While I believe you don't need a degree in psychology to be successful, being able to read a room and your clients is critically important to the entrepreneurial journey. I've had more than two decades of practice, and I still learn new ways to adapt my approach and to sharpen my radar to stay ahead of potential harm to my business. I trust my gut every single time.

By the way, it definitely helps to have a firm handshake, to look the other person in the eye, and to pay attention to the details. Apply these techniques in your next meeting, whether with internal stakeholders or in a client meeting. To reiterate again, success or failure often lies within the details.

IMPORTANT DETAILS

» Harness the power of your intuition and apply it in the workplace.

» Learn to read your clients and colleagues. Understand what motivates and resonates with them.

» Always trust your gut instinct.

CHAPTER EIGHT

⌒

ON ADVERSITY

The door to the office opened with a bang. It was nearly eight o'clock in the evening and I was the only person still in the office. I quickly saw that it was the facilities manager coming to empty our trash. I waved from my desk. He shouted good-bye to me on his way out. Being that our offices were at the end of the hallway, I knew he'd be wrapping up his day soon. Not wanting to be the last person in the building, I saved a version of the document I was working on and started to collect my belongings.

Just as I was getting up, I heard the door to the office suddenly swing open. "I'm leaving now," I instinctively shouted from my desk. Startled, I looked up to see my boss storming into my office. He was enraged. He threw his binder and padfolio onto my co-worker's desk and lunged toward me at my desk. He was yelling incoherently at the top of his lungs about a deal he just lost. I could only catch every other word but heard something about losing a million dollars. I slid back from my chair against the exterior glass wall, essentially trapped between the glass wall and him.

My hand shot over to the dial pad on the desk phone. I hit 911 on the keypad. My hand hovered there but I didn't place the call. I had the sudden realization that I was very much the only one in the office and that the facilities manager was not within earshot. By this point, my boss was screaming at me that I was a 26-year-old on a power trip, called me smug, told me that I didn't understand what it meant to be in his shoes. To this point, I had not uttered a word. My boss was known for having a temper and for using choice words when he didn't get his way, but I had never experienced this kind of over-the-top rage in my life. He continued to move toward me, backing me into a corner.

Instinctively, I went into survival mode. My adrenaline took over. I have no recollection of the exact words that I said. As I spoke, though, he started to calm down. I was reassuring him that it was going to be okay. I grabbed my purse and started to move slowly toward him in an attempt to slip around him to leave the office. I continued to tell him that it was getting late. Maybe a good night's sleep would put things into perspective. Maybe he could salvage the deal. I also explained that I needed to meet my roommate who was waiting on me to get home. As we reached the main door, he started to thank me for being so compassionate and for listening to him. He said he would drive me to my car. I insisted that I could easily walk out the front door to my car. He was parked in the garage, so it didn't make sense. But he insisted and led me into the garage.

I stayed calm even though I was terrified. The most outrageous thoughts ran through my head from being trapped in his car to someone finding my body in the river the next morning.

To stave off the panic, I gripped my keys so I could use them as a weapon if need be. We took the short drive to the front of the building. He told me he would be in New York City for the rest of the week, and he would call me from the road.

I quickly got into my car, sped out of the parking lot, and got onto the interstate. I started to cry uncontrollably. I pulled over on the side of the road when I was about five miles from the office on the berm of the highway. I called my dad. I was sobbing so hard; I could barely talk. My dad asked me if I was alright. I recounted what had just happened. He did his best to get me to calm down such that I could complete the 25-mile drive back to the suburbs of Philadelphia. He told me to rest if I could and that we would discuss the next steps in the morning.

"I was not fine. It was not fine. I didn't know if everything was going to be okay."

I barely slept. At seven o'clock the next morning, I called one of the board members requesting an impromptu meeting that day. Knowing that my boss was in NYC, I had a few days to get things sorted out and organized before his return. I met a few hours later with two board members where I recounted the details.

I asked the board members for assurances that my boss's behavior would be addressed so that myself and the staff were not put at risk like this again. The board members agreed that his angry behavior was a serious problem, one they had known about, and that they would address the concerns with him. They asked if I was going to sue them to which I replied, "No." I just wanted there to be better protocols in place to prevent this kind of situation from happening again.

We had decided in the meeting that moving forward, my team and I were to leave on time every day and under no circumstances would any of the team members be in the office alone, after normal business hours. Where possible, for the foreseeable future, I was not to have a meeting alone with my boss. I was appreciative of their assistance, but I did tell them that if this did happen again, we would have a very different conversation. They nodded and understood.

Within days, the board addressed the concerns with my boss directly. When he returned from New York City, my boss was profusely apologetic to the point of tears. At our event the following week, another board member approached me.

"Hey Julie, I heard what happened. You know how he is," he said, with a nervous laugh. "I was thinking about how much this reminds me of an episode of *Oprah*. You know, the one where the abused wife sits on the couch with the abusive husband?"

To say I was shocked is an understatement. An episode of *Oprah*?

"Do you have girls?" I asked.

"Yes, I have two; ages nine and 11. Why do you ask?" he said.

"I hope that one day your girls don't come to you with this type of situation. Somehow, I don't think you'll relate it to an episode of *Oprah*," I said directly to his face, as I then turned and walked away. It was as if I had to live through the horror again, knowing that some of the board members thought this was funny or just a minor co-workers' quarrel.

About a month or so after this incident, the office environment had been quiet and uneventful. It was as if nothing had ever happened. One morning, my boss casually asked me to meet him in the conference room for a quick meeting. My second-in-command at the time asked if I wanted her to join me. I told her that I should be okay but to definitely keep an eye out. The conference room was visible from our office.

The offices were all glass and very transparent to all. The conference room had glass on three sides, so you could see the entire room at any angle. As the meeting started, I positioned myself to take notes. Just as I looked up, my boss started screaming at me once again about the pressure he was under, how I was on a power trip, and that the board hated me. Again, I had not uttered a word. As he got louder, I looked to see another partner stand up behind his desk in response to the yelling. I could see my second-in-command come out of our office and put her hand on the doorknob.

"Let's regroup on this meeting at another time. Can you please let me by?" I calmly asked as I moved toward the door.

He blocked me and shouted, "Sit your ass back down. I will tell you when I am done with you!"

By this point, several partners were coming out of their offices, and my co-worker shoved the door so hard it knocked my boss out of the way. She grabbed my arm and pulled me out of the conference room. We grabbed my things and headed to a coffee shop to calm down. I tried to hold it together as best I could. I was shaking uncontrollably. At least this time, I had witnesses.

Two days later, I hired an attorney and started the process of negotiating my severance and exit package. After all, I had worked so hard to get this job and now I had to leave not because of anything I had done wrong, but because of a toxic, out-of-control boss. And of course, because I wasn't willing to subject myself to this abhorrent behavior.

When I met with my lawyer for the first time, I brought with me 20 pages of notes, front and back, detailing my experience working in this environment. I listed specific dates and times and noted who witnessed these events. I shared diary entries from the hard days and certainly the detailed notes from what I still consider one of the worst days of my career. My lawyer was stunned.

"What result are you looking for here, Julie?" he inquired. "I can walk you through the scenarios of pursuing legal action if that is the path you want to go down. You have a solid case and based on this evidence, you will win."

Until this point, I don't know that I had really considered what options I did have. I could have never imagined needing a lawyer at the age of 26. I knew that I was in an extremely toxic environment. I knew that the behavior and culture would not change even if he was no longer my direct boss. I was scared. I was angry. I solicited opinions from my lawyer, my family, and close friends. They were incredible listeners but, in the end, they didn't have an answer to what path I should choose.

No matter which choice, to walk away with severance or to pursue legal action, it was career suicide. In this industry, women weren't even a significant minority in the room. To be 26 years old, I knew how the narrative would likely play out. I didn't want to be the girl who went from being featured in the *Philadelphia Business Journal* to being painted as a girl who couldn't hack it.

I opted to not pursue the path of litigation. I decided that a severance package would at a minimum provide what I needed to move forward.

I was extremely fair in my request. My lawyer even suggested that I was being too fair. I ended up getting everything that I had asked for, including a glowing letter of recommendation from the board of directors. They were as apologetic as they could be, knowing that they were complicit. I'd later learn this had happened to previous employees before me. I was the only one to draw a hard line in the sand.

I was 26. My dream job suddenly turned out to be one of the worst experiences I'd ever had to this point in my life. To me this was like a death. I was fully mourning a career I had worked so hard to build. I was now faced with starting over again. I knew my old boss would prevent me from working in the venture capital environment, even though we had a contract. That is how he operated. I had seen him do it to others.

During the first few weeks, post this experience, I tried to decompress before thinking through the next step in my career.

As a young professional, I didn't expect to enter a workforce only to be met with what is considered verbal abuse or even the fear of physical violence. I didn't expect the response from colleagues who likened this experience to daytime television. As a motivated, young, female professional, I did expect to work long hours, receive little or no praise, and to be met with critical feedback as to how I could improve my performance. After having worked in a restaurant, I romanticized what work would look like in a "professional" environment. But I was completely and totally unprepared for this experience. While I navigated it the best I could, it was an experience that I have not forgotten and one that has continued to haunt me as I moved on in my career.

When future business would take me to Philadelphia or the surrounding area, I would instinctively fear bumping into my old boss or any of the board members. It wasn't until I had learned of my former boss's passing that I realized the grip this experience had on me, years later when I was the CEO of my own firm.

As I would learn, future work environments often proved to have even looser protocols and terrible mismanagement from top to bottom. I developed a tougher skin, armed to take on unforeseen challenges. For me, this experience was a profound lesson. It made me tougher and likely should have made me angry. Instead, it reaffirmed that I never wanted to experience this again. It is what ultimately pushed me down the path to launching my business and establishing a better environment. That is exactly what I did.

"Well, Julie, you have to understand...my business partner gets the sense that this business of yours—Junction Creative—that it's just a hobby for you."

I was stunned by this. And it was said to my face by a longtime client of Junction's, as he walked me to the elevator after a tense management meeting.

"A hobby?? You are my smallest client in terms of revenue and budget," I fumed under my breath. Regardless, it was the very last thing I would have expected to hear from this client.

We exchanged good-byes as I hopped onto the elevator. I put my sunglasses on just as the tears started to roll down my face.

This client was one of Junction's very first clients. The client was also a start-up. We assisted his company with a business plan, sales model, marketing plan, company name, branding, logo, website, content development, sales presentations, social media management, public relations, and even assisted with the hiring of their internal sales team. I provided executive consulting on a regular basis, working with the partners to launch and to grow the business. As with any client, I cared deeply about the success of the company, even to the point where one of the partners said that I cared more about the business than they did. I was just as passionate about doing the work as I was about delivering results.

We had established the collective goals of the partners during the business planning process. We developed a strategy to map those goals. Knowing what the end goal looked like, we were then able to put in place the right people, systems, and documentation to prepare this company. And I delivered just that. When the client was being targeted by a larger, soon to be publicly traded company for acquisition, much of the documentation that was required for due diligence was already prepared.

After having worked for seven years to grow this client's business, I was excited to see their dreams come to fruition. My firm was not in the business of mergers and acquisitions, but my business background provided strong capabilities to prepare this client for the process. This was a great case study for Junction, proving that we can do exactly what we say we do and exactly how we say we will do it.

As the negotiations continued between the partners and the CEO of the other company, the one partner would send me all his emails to get my review, feedback, and edits before sending back to the CEO. During a once-in-a-lifetime vacation to Sir Richard Branson's Necker Island, in the British Virgin Islands, he even called me asking for assistance in getting responses back to the CEO. I immediately jumped in, despite interrupting an extraordinary vacation.

When I returned from my trip, I attended one of our standing management meetings to review the progress over the last week. I laid out the next steps for moving this deal forward. I introduced them to an M&A expert who I had worked with on previous deals, someone I trusted. If you aren't familiar with the M&A process, these firms take a percentage of the deal. I wanted to be sure that the partners were in the best hands. One partner knew a gentleman from his personal life who was part of a M&A group. I was then told during this meeting that they already hired this other fellow. Knowing a little about this other firm, I just warned them against hiring a M&A group that requires money up front or takes escalating fees.

In this same meeting, another partner became agitated with me. It was out of character for him. He ended up walking out of the meeting early, and in a huff. He said that he was "sick and tired of me always pointing out the negative." I was merely sharing my knowledge and experience in working with these firms and how to read the contracts. I happened to also know that this gentleman and his team were recently fired from a notable M&A firm and were currently without a home, so to speak. I didn't share this with the team as I had only heard this information secondhand through a colleague who worked with them directly. It wasn't public knowledge and I had received this information in confidence. In short, I was protecting my client without violating my promise to not disclose this information.

I was rattled at the level of anger coming from this partner. I reiterated to the team that my goal was to make this a successful exit. I would happily step aside if they felt I was no longer needed. After all, I was not going to profit from this deal in any way. Outside of my monthly fees, which I would lose once they were acquired, I didn't have a dollar on the line.

From the look on the other partners' faces, they had no idea what had happened. They apologized for his behavior after he left and thanked me for all the hard work and dedication that I had put in over the last seven years. A few minutes later, the other partner said he'd walk me to the elevator.

A hobby? Is that really what this boiled down to? In the weeks and months that followed, I would revisit this conversation over and over again in my head. I questioned whether it was because I was a female. Would he have said this to a male counterpart? Was I too negative in these meetings? Did I somehow offend this partner without realizing it? A hobby? On face value, the comment was ridiculous. But it hurt, a lot. Still does, if you catch me on a bad day. Seven years of work, consistent effort, and results to show for it and I was reduced to someone who did this for a hobby.

Like many times before, I didn't see it coming. And even if I saw it coming, I don't know that I would have been better prepared. The client went on to sell the company for the exact amount they were looking to receive, as outlined in the original business plan. The business plan that I wrote. I was even invited to the celebratory dinner with the M&A firm and the partners once the deal had finally closed. What they didn't know is that I forced myself to go to this dinner. I was sick to my stomach as they toasted their incredible success, and when the M&A gentleman said that there wasn't a whole lot for him to really do, seeing that the work had already been done by me. He shared his sincere appreciation for my contribution. I said "thank you" as I smiled and choked down my wine.

I am sure you are wondering why I would even go to this dinner. In the end, I knew that I was an integral part of this business and its success. I showed up for seven years, from the initial business plan meeting to this celebratory dinner. While I will never know which partner said that this was a hobby for me, I also knew the truth. And I wasn't going to let that insulting comment derail the progress I had made with my own business or overshadow the incredible value I provided to this company. I dusted off my ego. I'd survived worse in my tenure as Junction's CEO.

Let me explain.

During this seven-year stretch with this client, totally unbeknownst to them or to any other client, I had experienced one of the worst setbacks in my own business since losing our seven-figure client in year three. What I had survived was much worse; I would certainly be able to move on after this bump in the road.

What was this terrible setback, you ask?

Since the age of 32, my husband and I were trying to start our family. During the process, doctors discovered that I had a noncancerous tumor that was preventing me from successfully carrying a child. I underwent an invasive surgery to remove the tumor in the hopes of being able to carry my own child. After I recovered, we resumed in vitro fertilization (IVF) to assist in the process. Because of the scar tissue and my age (yes, 35 is considered geriatric), I was considered high risk for complications.

Over the course of three years, I gave myself over 400 shots, underwent numerous fertility procedures, and miscarried so many times. After so many failed attempts, we started the process for adoption, as I was committed to starting a family, no matter where the child came from. Physically, I had reached a point where I could no longer handle the side effects of the drugs. My body was breaking down. It was emotionally and physically taxing. It was a very dark time.

And yet, during all of this, I still showed up at work every day. I didn't share any of these personal struggles with the team or my clients. It was business as usual. Work kept my mind focused on something other than needles and heartbreak. I was able to set goals and to accomplish them without much struggle.

In the winter/spring of 2014, we were overjoyed to learn that we were pregnant with twins. Our last round of IVF, successful! The doctor wanted to be sure that I understood what the next 37 weeks would look like. I was to prepare myself for a high-risk pregnancy. No working out. No stress. Absolutely no changes in blood pressure. If possible, I was to walk no more than 100 yards per day as the pregnancy progressed. I was to monitor my blood pressure, attend regular scans, and continue with the hormone shots until week 12. No caffeine. And most important, no stress. Not even a little bit.

I remember leaving the doctor's office elated at the good news but also grounded by the reality and severity of this situation.

Junction was my labor of love, my first child, so to say. It had been my sole focus for the last seven years. No stress? How was that going to work? In the weeks that followed, I was faced with what felt like an impossible challenge and what felt like an unfair choice. Having struggled for years to reach this incredible milestone in my personal life, I had to make the right decision to protect my family, even if that meant sacrificing the business.

Ultimately, I made the decision to downsize the team, running as lean as we possibly could, while still being able to deliver for our clients. I kept our retainer-based accounts but would not focus on bringing on any new clients until after my pregnancy. It felt like the death of a dream, even though we were still in business. I had to let go of incredible people who were great at their jobs and who I considered friends. It was the one time in my career that I lost my composure and cried openly in front of the team. I didn't disclose the full reasons that I was downsizing, rather just communicated that the business could not support a larger team. It was a loss that would take me years to recover from. I felt like a complete failure.

I suffered in silence. Our clients had no idea that we had reduced the team. In fact, they didn't even know that I was pregnant until I was six months along. There were many days that I stared at the wall in my office, accepting what I considered a mediocre path in the history of my business. It might have slowed me down, but I wasn't out. After my beautiful babies were born, I built Junction back, client by client, dollar by dollar, achieving milestones I never thought we'd reach.

Adversity in business comes in various forms. It could be financial ruin, health problems, dishonest employees, natural disasters, or global pandemics.

But if there is one universal truth about adversity, it definitely is out there, and for the vast majority of entrepreneurs, they will encounter adversity at one point or another in their career. The key to surviving any kind of setback is to embrace it and cope with it. And don't panic.

The impact of COVID-19 on business owners proved that no one person will be exempt from experiencing adversity. When it does happen, unexpectedly in most cases, I am not suggesting that it be ignored. Regardless of the circumstance or situation, you can either choose to let it be the only part of your story or you can let it become just a chapter. When you face the unthinkable or the insurmountable in your business, don't give up, focus forward, and let it be a stepping stone for what is to come next.

It's been said that adversity is a great equalizer. It's not what happens to you but how you respond to it. Adversity in my career has proved to be a valuable part of my journey as an entrepreneur. I am reminded of my 26-year-old self. I was fearless and a little less aware of how harsh the world could be. But I woke up every day, put one foot in front of the other, and never let adversity stop me in my tracks. The experiences, while traumatic, made me more resolute in what I knew business could be. I became a better version of myself. I built confidence. I learned how to think beyond the circumstance and crawl forward stronger, and just a little braver, than before.

IMPORTANT DETAILS

» It's almost certain that every entrepreneur will face uncertainty. It is a great equalizer.

» You may not be prepared to face adversity, but it's how you respond that builds character.

» Let those challenging moments shape your way forward.

CHAPTER NINE

‿

WORK/LIFE BALANCE

"Ugh, I am so late," I gasped as I raced to my car. I flung my work bag, missing the front seat, and all its contents fell onto the floor of the car.

I sped out of the parking lot en route to my girls' preschool Christmas recital. The school was just a half mile from my office. As I pulled into the parking lot, I was pleasantly surprised at how many parking spots were still available. I was expecting to have to park across the street.

I grabbed my cell phone, leaving my purse and all of its contents behind. I ran across the parking lot to the front of the building. I reached for the double door to the auditorium only to find that it was locked. How could the doors be locked? I quickly pulled up my phone to check my calendar—only to realize that I was in fact 45 minutes late! In my desperate rush, I had looked at my calendar incorrectly. Paralyzed for a minute, I stood there staring at the locked door. Tears stung my cheeks as I walked back to the main school entrance. I work literally half a mile away, a four-minute drive from the office to the school, and I missed the girls' entire performance.

As I entered the holiday party in the classroom, both of my four-year-old daughters looked at me in surprise. I reached down to hug them, and they asked, "Where were you, Mommy?" It took all that I had to not break down in front of the entire classroom, full of parents and children. After the party was over, I made my way back to the office to finish the workday. Feeling like a complete failure, I was less than productive for the rest of the day. I certainly lost my chance of winning Mother of the Year.

Rewind to 2014 when I was pregnant with my twin daughters. I had it all planned. The babies were due the week of Christmas. Our offices were closed the week between Christmas and New Year's Day, which gave me at least two weeks to recover. At the time, my sister was managing most of our accounts so I would have a little more flexibility in the schedule at the start of the New Year. With a high-risk twin-pregnancy, I was scheduled for a C-section that would come with a six-week recovery period to get back on my feet. Most of my work was done on the computer and over the phone, so I planned to be able to return to work before the six weeks was over.

I clearly remember getting eye rolls and whispers when I would tell others of my noble plans to return to work on a prompt and efficient basis.

It was irritating to hear others tell me that I should expect to stop working altogether or to put aside my small business until after my girls were old enough for school. The nerve of them to suggest such a thing! From my perspective, I was extremely organized. If I can build a business and run a household, I can surely add children into the mix. Why couldn't I have both? It wasn't until the day that my daughters arrived that I came face-to-face with the major life shift that was about to happen.

Over the holidays, I thought I could easily adjust to the role in caring for two babies who were completely incapable of caring for themselves. Wow, was I wrong!

I had spreadsheets to manage feedings, diaper changes, and sleep schedules. Those plans didn't last very long. Thank goodness, my mom agreed to stay for a few weeks as I did my best to get used to two brand-new little people in my family. But in those early weeks, I finally realized, quite understandably, that the bulk of the responsibility would fall on me to take care of the girls. I was the keeper of the doctor appointments, feedings, diaper changes, and all things baby x 2.

While I love a great project plan, being a mom was so much greater than any other life challenge I'd ever tackled. I slept very little. The exhaustion was like nothing I have ever experienced. Four weeks passed within the blink of an eye.

Every entrepreneur will face a different scenario for how to manage a business while also raising children. For Steve and me, we agreed that we would need to hire a nanny to help us with the girls. We live hundreds of miles from our closest family members, and we wanted to have the girls in our home as opposed to a daycare. While Steve worked from home, he had an intense work travel schedule. If our girls were at home, I would still be able to see them if I wanted to during the day. At the end of the day, you have to make the best decision for your family. It's clearly an important and very personal decision.

By mid-January, I started back at work but only half days. I would head to my office in the basement around nine in the morning and work as many hours as I could that day. I looked forward to heading downstairs into the office. I must confess that, looking back, work provided an outlet. A time during each day where I felt like I could control something whether it was an email or discussing a marketing strategy. I knew how to be effective at my job. I was struggling to find my way as a new mom, a wife, and as a CEO.

"I'm not fine. It will be fine. Everything will be fine?"

In the early days of Junction, I was married with no children. My husband and I both worked long hours on our businesses. It would not be unlike us to be working late into the evening or on a Sunday afternoon. I was accessible and available to my clients at any time. But deep down, I also knew that when we started to have kids, it would be incredibly important to me to find a real equilibrium, prioritizing my family while also balancing the demands of the business.

⌒⌒

I was raised by a working mom, who made it look so effortless and easy. When I was in high school, the alarm would go off at six in the morning. I would hear my mom moving around in the kitchen, making coffee and preparing her breakfast. By the time I made it to the kitchen, she had already read a chapter in her book and made her to-do lists for the day. I would quickly get myself ready for school. She would either drop me at the bus stop at the end of our neighborhood or she'd often offer to drive me to school, before starting her 20-minute commute to work in the opposite direction. When she arrived home later that day at 3:30, she would go downstairs, sit in the recliner, and take a 20-minute catnap. That is, of course, if I didn't have a game for her to attend. Around 4:30, she'd quickly change into the Avenue uniform and head into the restaurant to give my dad a break and then assist in closing the restaurant around 9pm.

After long days at the restaurant, my family and I would go to our favorite pizza shop and sit in our favorite booth. We sat in silence, staring at each other, until our food order was ready. As we comforted ourselves with pizza and subs, one comment about the day turned into a conversation as to what went wrong that day, what needed to be done before we opened the next day, and who was responsible for what. By the time we had revisited and rehashed the entire 14-hour day, it was nearly ten o'clock. My parents would head to the bank to drop off the deposit. My sister and I would stop at the local grocery store to pick up any food items that we needed. By the time we got home, I'd shower, do any homework, and get ready for bed.

When my dad and mom bought the restaurant, it was decided that the restaurant would be his full-time focus. My mom would keep her current job for a couple of reasons. The medical benefits were great and to this point, my parents hadn't worked together, full-time. My dad would no longer be traveling for work. Balance would be restored to the family... Or so we thought! We accepted this intense schedule as the daily routine, seven days a week. As a teenager, I was solely focused on how this schedule affected my social life. I also knew that college was in my near future, offering a break from this routine. As a daughter, I felt sympathy for my mom. She didn't get a break. I knew there were days when she likely wanted to stay in the recliner and read her book until bedtime. I knew she was likely angry and exhausted. And for years, my dad received a lot of the accolades for the business success at the Avenue as my mom stood quietly in the background.

As the business grew, so did the intensity. Even though my parents had great employees, they were never able to break away for a few days from the business. It was always the primary focus. We joked about finding balance but knew it was a lofty goal. At the time, I could never really understand why they worked themselves to the bone without taking time for themselves to rest. It was difficult to watch the most important people in your life work so hard, with very little opportunity to relish in their success.

I too struggled to find the balance in those early years working for my parents. When I moved to Philadelphia, I still carried a fair amount of guilt that I was now charting my own path and wasn't actively contributing to the family business. I was vocal to my family that if this is what owning a business was like, I wasn't interested. That is, if I worked for someone else, I could leave work at the end of the day and just enjoy my 20s.

What I soon learned is that this concept of "work/life balance" was really just ethereal, just something people talked about and desperately searched for. As a young professional, when starting my career, I worked long days, took work home, and spent most evenings at a networking event trying to build my influence. I received only five vacation days in my first year. And because I was the newest member of the team, I was expected to work Christmas Eve until 4pm and be back in the office first thing on December 26. Little changed, even as I was promoted or recruited to join new organizations. If I wanted to be successful in business, I had to sacrifice my personal life for the company I was working for with little control over my future endeavors.

I understood better, why my parents made the decision to invest in themselves. My motivation for starting Junction wasn't an attempt to find work/life balance, but rather an opportunity to invest in myself. This is an important distinction that every entrepreneur or business owner needs to understand.

Over the last decade, I've inched closer to achieving my vision for work/life balance. Getting closer to the goal was a lot harder than I had imagined. It evolves just as the business does. Here are a few of the most important lessons I've learned along the way.

CREATE A SCHEDULE

Many of you will face an ever-present challenge to establish a structure or schedule for yourself. Whether you start a business before you've started a family or years after you've launched, you need to find a way to structure your days in a way that meets the demands of both. I often flash back to the days when I saw my mom napping on her recliner before starting her second work shift of the day. As a working mom myself, my appreciation for her only grew. I now understood what she felt. And yet, she always had time for a laugh, a hug, or ten minutes to listen to me talk about my day. If I was going to survive, I knew that I had to find a way to make this work so that I could be present with my children, my family, while also staying true to myself. It was a bumpy road to walk down. I tried to think through the ideal schedule. Inspired by my twin spreadsheets, I realized that I needed my own schedule to follow. I would wake up at six in the morning when the kids woke up so that I could spend time with them in the morning. Around 8:30am, I would shower and get ready. By nine, I would head down to the office to start the morning. At lunchtime, I would head upstairs and spend about 30 minutes with the girls before returning to work. At 5pm, I would squeeze in a workout for 45 minutes. Our nanny would leave at 6pm, so that I could spend a couple of hours with the girls before their bedtime. If I was lucky, they would be in bed by 7:30pm or 8pm without stirring until midnight.

The trick was to be present, whether at work or with my kids. If I was at work, I did my best to not get distracted by the sounds I would hear coming from upstairs. If I heard one of the girls crying, I would sometimes bring one down with me, to sit on my lap, as I worked. After work, I would put my phone away so that I wasn't distracted by emails or phone calls. On the weekends, I didn't check my work email until Sunday evening after the girls went to bed.

The hours were slow, but the years were quick. This schedule allowed me the flexibility to be with my girls when I wanted or needed to be. It also allowed me to remain dedicated to my business. There were days where I held the girls a little longer or missed a bedtime due to work travel. Remember: every day is exhausting. I am reminded that while this might not be considered a true "balance," this is my way of having both, work and life. And it worked for me.

In the process of finding my own path forward as a CEO, I realized the importance of creating an environment for my employees that provided a similar benefit.

> » I give employees the option to choose whether they work 8am-5pm or 9am-6pm. I just ask that they pick one option and that they are consistent with it.

> » I don't require employees to use PTO (Paid Time Off) days for doctor's appointments, children's sickness, etc. I completely understand that "life happens" and sometimes between the hours of 8am and 6pm. If the privilege is abused, reserve the right to modify the policy.

> » I close the Junction offices from December 24 through January 1 so that employees can spend time with their families. We prepare in advance so that our clients are aware of the schedule and that if an emergency arises, I am always available.

> » I encourage the team to get to work on time, work hard, and leave on time. No need to have to stay late.

> » I don't allow clients to text our team members.

> » All email or phone communication stops at 5:30pm, Monday through Friday, unless there is an emergency.

I recognize how hard it is to manage work and life, especially with the addition of children. In my previous work experience, the environments I worked in would log employees' time, monitor lunch breaks, and expect you to work even when sick. And I recognize that the work environment and expectations have now shifted with the rise of the millennials and Generation Z. While we aren't playing Ping-Pong and drinking beer for happy hour at the office, my team is getting the work done so they can always leave on time, every day.

But in truth, it's still a struggle.

This quest to reach work/life balance can be futile. I've yet to speak to an entrepreneur who has achieved true equilibrium. I've read the books, the blogs, the social media posts, and research articles on how to have it all. But I've learned from hard experience that as an entrepreneur and a parent that it's pretty much impossible to have it all at one time. You will be forced to sacrifice one for the other in certain situations. At the end of the day though, I am mindful of the fact that I get to make these personal choices to invest my time where I need to, whether as a room mom at my daughters' school or as a CEO.

COMMON GROUND

Some years ago, a colleague of mine said that he puts little expectations on employees who are getting married, suffered a loss, or having a baby. "With life events, you can't really expect anything from a person, as their entire focus is on the life event."

I remember looking at him and saying, "Well, I am getting married in a month and I am still showing up for work."

"Yes, but I don't expect for you to accomplish anything," he responded.

At the time, I had a few choice words for his assessment that I muttered on the walk back to my office. He was married, with children, and had recently lost a family member. How would he feel if I said that I expected that he contributed nothing to the team?

As a business owner, I have to confess that my attitude shifted on this a bit. That is, I would later learn that there was some truth to his statement, albeit he communicated it poorly. When any person is faced with a life event, whether positive or negative, it consumes our personal lives. It is an ever-present thought throughout our days. During these times, our professional life takes a back seat to what is being required of us. It's not intentional. It's just reality for most employees.

I think that's probably a fair assessment. Although I do think that when it's your company, when you're the entrepreneur, it's much more likely that you will always continue to put as much effort as possible into your day-to-day business affairs. But when it's one of your employees, you have to understand that they are probably not as emotionally invested in your firm as you are.

As a business owner, you have to be prepared to manage these life events fairly so as to not create possible dissension among your team. For example, our business policies formally dictate how many personal days are offered in the event that a close family member should pass away. The policies are designed to offer each employee the same benefit. However, in reality, as a leader you will evaluate each situation on a case-by-case basis. Policies aren't designed to enforce empathy. My dad used to tell me,

"CEOs and employees start the day the same way... by putting one pants leg on at a time." Meaning that, at the end of the day, we are all humans. This notion has stuck with me since I worked at the Avenue. No one person is more important than another person. No one situation is worse or better than the next. And it's okay to show empathy.

In my professional experience, I remember the few times that I needed to request a day off to attend a funeral or doctor's appointment. When I did ask, I was usually met with a list of the things that I needed to accomplish if I was to leave for an extra hour. I was encouraged to use my lunch hour to make doctor's appointments or make the phone calls to schedule an appointment. It always felt a little like the children's game "Mother, may I..."

I started my business at the age of 30. I didn't have children or aging parents to take care of. I had a much greater appreciation for owning my own business as I shuffled with daily IVF appointments, surgery, having twins, and doctor's appointments for three people instead of just myself. I often wondered how I would have been able to manage if I was still working for someone else's company. Would I have been met with empathy? Likely, not.

This perspective taught me to recognize that we are all on common ground when it comes to life, death, and other life events. My sister Marci will tell you that I am empathetic at my core. When an employee is facing an illness or a personal matter and needs time off, I rarely, if ever, say no to such a request. I also know from experience that appointments take longer than an hour, always. Weddings and babies require a lot of preparation and appointments that almost never fall outside of traditional work hours. And we know that grieving a loved one can sometimes take longer than three business days. As a result of COVID-19 protocols, parents were being tasked to teach their children at home while also carrying the responsibilities of a full-time job.

When faced with challenges like these, I reassure the employee that we can handle their job responsibilities so they can focus on what is needed. Having learned from my parents, I step up and step in, rolling up my sleeves to help with the workload so the rest of the team isn't feeling overwhelmed by the absence.

RELAX. RELATE. RELEASE. LET GO. LET FLOW.

My co-worker would often walk through the office chanting his mantra "Relax, relate, release. Let go, let flow." Odd as it may seem, I'd take a deep breath in and smile as I exhaled. It was a simple, yet effective way to release tension or to pause in a chaotic moment. Nearly 15 years later, I still repeat this mantra under my breath in times when the pressure seems to be boiling over.

As an employee, if I had a particularly bad day at the office, I would leave the office and regroup in time for my return to the office the next day. I would commiserate with co-workers at happy hour or dinner. We would avow that we would put on a happy face and slog through it together. We supported each other and provided a safe space in the event that our favorite mantra didn't do the trick.

But as an entrepreneur, you don't have the ability to walk away and leave the problems at the office. The business will follow you home and will rise and fall with you.

"Where did your dad go?" the chef asked as I walked into the restaurant.

"I have no idea, I just got here," I said, somewhat annoyed that I had not even crossed the threshold of the back door before being asked where my dad was. How should I know where he is? This was before apps like Life360 and tracking capabilities on our cell phones. I made my way through the kitchen into the dining room to start my shift.

"Good afternoon!" I said as I greeted the waitresses.

"Hi Julie, do you know where your dad went?" one of the waitresses replied.

"No, I literally just walked in. Do you need something?" I asked. What on earth is going on here? I was beginning to think that I missed something important.

"Well, not really. I just wanted to tell him that I was thinking about taking vacation in like six months and wanted to see if he had done the schedule yet. I also wanted to ask him if he was going to get some more bananas. We need bananas for the breakfast shift tomorrow. And we will need coleslaw in a couple of days, so I didn't know if he knew that."

In other words, this was all just a bunch of nonurgent routine questions.

As I stood there, I had a sneaking suspicion that my dad had left the building. My dad had a habit of walking to the bank midday to either get change for the cash register or to make a deposit. It was only about a half a mile each way to the bank, so it could take around 20 minutes unless he stopped to speak to other business owners on his route. It was his time to get a break from the restaurant and the staff. Based on my greeting on this particular day, he had likely slipped out. The questions from the staff were not pressing and honestly could have been communicated to other staff members to resolve. My dad didn't need to tell the chef to make coleslaw. The waitress could have walked back into the kitchen, as she had done no less than 100 times, that very shift. If my dad would have told them he was walking to the bank, he would have been met with this barrage of questions.

If you've ever managed a team of people, a business, or even a household with children, you know that with the title comes the responsibility of fielding questions for much of the day. I would always chuckle when my dad walked to the bank. If he told me where he was going, I knew there was an actual need to go to the bank. If he didn't, he was escaping, even if only for 20 minutes that afternoon.

It wasn't until I started growing my business that I realized how valuable those "walks to the bank" must have been for my dad. I was working long hours, dreaming about the business, and waking up with the very same issues or problems that I faced the day before. In order to avoid burnout, I gave myself 60 minutes a day to go for a run. Much like I scheduled my meetings, I would include the workout on my agenda, giving it equal importance to all the other tasks on my list. Over the years, I have found that, in terms of work/life balance, I really need to have that hour each day to be able to clear my mind. Yes, it's that important. As you embark on the entrepreneurial journey, find the one activity that allows you to breathe easy, clear your mind, or just be you for one hour a day. Find an outlet to allow yourself to let go of whatever is weighing on your mind.

As busy entrepreneurs, we sometimes forget to give ourselves permission to take a break. And know that it's okay to get frustrated with clients or colleagues. It's okay if you need to take some time to clear your head. It's okay to be human. We expect so much of ourselves, all day, every day.

Allow yourself at least one hour a day to be you. Leave the responsibility, the work, the employees, the financial worries behind. All of this will be waiting for you until you return. And I promise, you will be better equipped to handle it.

I wish I could tell you that if you create a schedule, find common ground, and relax a little that you will find the right work/life balance. I know this is what helped me as I navigated my way through it all. And if all else fails, I remind myself that sometimes investing in yourself requires a little more than you've bargained for. And in the end, it's worth it.

IMPORTANT DETAILS

» Define and think about what work/life balance means for you.

» Life happens when you least expect it. Do the best you can to adjust and adapt.

» Strive for balance in your life and in your work. But don't be disappointed when it looks different than you thought it would.

CHAPTER TEN

⌒⌐

ACCOUNTABILITY & RESPONSIBILITY

It was 6pm. I was in my 20s and working at the agency with the business development team and the account team on a large Request for Proposal (RFP) for a Fortune 500 beverage company. Our response to the RFP was due by 6pm PST. Back in 2007, most companies would still require a printed copy of your response as opposed to an email attachment. We needed to get the printed copies to the FedEx for Same Day by 7pm ET to reach the destination. To say we were cutting it close is a complete understatement.

Four of us were working on the final drafts. I was the third reviewer of each document with my immediate manager being the final reviewer before printing. The CEO finished up his introductory letter and it eventually made it to my attention for review. Understanding the importance of reviewing the CEO's content for fear that someone would overlook my changes, I not only tracked the changes but also highlighted the text changes in yellow. I added a note in the margin with the original and my suggested changes. I then emailed the document to my direct manager, his direct boss, and the CEO with a note detailing what edits were made, and to reference the highlighted tracked changes. I then walked into my direct manager's office and told him to review my notes before accepting the changes, as I had made notes. He acknowledged me by saying that he would be sure to review all my notes before signing off on the letter.

Just before 7pm ET, the documents were taken to FedEx (across the street) and mailed. The team was proud of the response and certainly excited at the opportunity to be selected to move forward in the RFP selection process. Completely exhausted, I made it home just before 8pm.

The next morning, I felt good about what we had accomplished and the Herculean efforts that went into getting the RFP out on time. When I got to work, the office was quiet, almost hushed that morning. As I sat down, I could see inter-office messages from a few colleagues asking what had happened. I had obviously missed something just before arriving that morning. What could have possibly happened between 8pm the night before and 10am the next day?

The CFO, my manager, and his boss were all in the CEO's office for what felt like an eternity. All three of them exited exasperated and the CEO slammed the door, hard, as they walked out. Those of us with sight line to the CEO's office just put our heads down and tried to work in complete silence.

Around 11am, I walked past my manager's office to let him know I was going to grab lunch.

"Can you come in and close the door for a minute?" he asked.

"Sure," I replied as I closed the door and sat down. "Is everything okay? Why is the CEO so angry?"

Nothing could have aptly prepared me for his response. "You. You are the reason why he's so pissed," he replied aggressively. I could feel the color drain from my face and my cheeks start to burn. Confused, I was replaying in my head what I could have possibly done to warrant doors slamming and yelling for nearly three hours. He then said, "Who do you think you are?" I blankly stared at him. "Who do you think you are to make edits to a letter that he wrote for this RFP? Why would you make edits?"

I quickly replied by saying that I was asked directly by him and his boss to review and edit the letter before it went into the RFP. I reminded him that I emailed all three of them, provided notes, highlighted the two individual changes, etc.

He cut me off before I could finish. "I didn't read your notes. I just uploaded it into the document so that we could get the RFP out. I don't really know what to do here, Julie. If I were you, avoid the CEO for the next few days and don't be surprised if you lose your job over this. I can't help you."

I felt the tears start to well up in my eyes, nodded, and asked to be excused for lunch. I spent the next 30 minutes driving around, crying uncontrollably. The thought that a few edits could invoke such a response was mind-blowing. To lose my job for completing tasks that were assigned to me was incomprehensible. I was so embarrassed for making the two edits, but I did what I thought I was tasked to do.

I finally pulled myself together and walked back into the office. It was in this moment that I made a choice to not just take responsibility but also take accountability for my actions—even at the risk of losing my job.

I walked to the CEO's office. His door was open. His head was down, staring at the computer. I gently knocked and asked if I could speak to him for a few minutes. He waved me in, without looking up, and asked me to shut the door.

He peered over his trendy, black-rimmed glasses and asked directly, "What?"

"I understand that you are upset with me because of the edits I made to your introductory letter. I greatly respect you and the company. I wanted to take this opportunity to apologize for making any edits to the letter that would result in losing this incredible opportunity for the firm," I said. I went on to apologize some more and reiterated the process that I had followed to avoid this very situation. However, I had edited the document. It was my responsibility, and I should be held accountable. *I was directly asked to review and make edits to the letter, which is what I did. I took various steps to ensure that the CEO, the senior vice president, and my boss were all aware of what changes I did make.* My intention was to improve the letter with edits as I found two instances where the client could potentially misread the CEO's intent. Nevertheless, I said that it would never happen again, and I hoped that he could accept my sincerest apologies.

He sat back in his chair, speechless. After what felt like minutes, he thanked me and said that he appreciated me coming into speak with him. I nodded and walked out of his office.

That was a tough day. I didn't lose my job. Although, I do wonder if I would have, had I not gone into his office. In most situations, you have a choice to be responsible and accountable. In this situation, I took both.

All these years later, I can still remember how I felt that day. I remember losing respect for my boss and his boss, as leaders, for not only shirking their responsibility but also their accountability in this situation. Their inaction was representative of the fact that despite having their titles, they had not learned the importance of either. If I had not spoken to the CEO, I would have likely lost my job. My manager made it clear that he was not going to help me. Rather, he was resigned to just let things transpire as they would. Knowing my direct manager was apathetic to my situation was a very harsh reality to face.

Accountability and responsibility are often used synonymously, yet the difference between the two is rarely understood. Accountability is defined by the duty to a set of tasks where the focus is on results. Responsibility is the duty to complete those tasks—so it is task driven, ongoing, and within one person's power or control. To clearly outline the difference, let's take a simple application. I am *responsible* for ordering the office supplies and snacks for the entire office. And, if the supplies and snacks run out, not only am I responsible, but I am held fully accountable as well. As an entrepreneur, not only must you understand how responsibility and accountability are different but also very much connected to each other. As the boss, you must accept that you will carry the burden of both. You will always be accountable or responsible to yourself, your employees, and your clients, albeit sometimes in different ways.

In my experience working in a family business, I was all too familiar with how the lines of accountability and responsibility were often blurred. As a waitress, I was responsible for doing my job including the various tasks that were assigned to me on each shift. As the boss's daughter, I was accountable to the family and the goals that my parents had set for the business whether I wanted to be or not. While the job was a source of stress as a teenager, it was the perfect training ground to not just understand what it meant to be accountable and responsible, but how the lack of both can affect an organization.

"You should come," the kitchen manager retorted as I walked through the kitchen after my shift was over.

"I don't know. I'll check with Marci. Thanks for the invite though!" I said.

The kitchen manager was known for organizing get-togethers after work with other employees. As the boss's daughters, Marci and I were careful not to hang out regularly with the staff after hours. It wasn't a hard-and-fast rule, just a boundary that we set for ourselves. It was often perceived that Marci and I were too good to hang out with the team, so on this rare occasion, we agreed to stop by.

As we walked into the kitchen manager's house, we immediately looked at each other, with a fear as to how we were going to get ourselves out of there. The entire kitchen team was there, less one or two folks, including the 14-year-old dishwashers. As we scanned the room, cigarettes, beer, and alcohol were lying around. The kitchen manager was even serving the teenagers alcohol. My sister was 21, but I was 19.

Marci and I, both quick on our feet, made up some believable story about forgetting to drop a deposit at the bank or needing to get to the store before it closed. We then left the party, silent. We knew, as Marci drove me home, that we needed to share this with our parents...and we would likely be called tattletales by the rest of the kitchen staff. We knew my parents' firm stance on this situation, and it was not going to result in a casual conversation.

Marci and I were sick to our stomachs as we told my parents what we had witnessed. We knew that this had ramifications far beyond just a few drinks at a co-worker's house. We lived in a small town. News traveled fast, even faster if you were considered a reputable person in the community. I clearly remember my dad saying, "It's not what you know, it's when you know it." We knew the risks in telling our parents what was happening. Our intent was not to get these employees in trouble, but rather to protect my parents from any potential issues that could arise at the hands of this employee.

As a manager of a staff, many of whom were considered legal minors, the kitchen manager was held responsible for managing this team and accountable to my parents for his performance. What he failed to understand in this situation is that his responsibilities didn't stop at the end of his shift. As a person in leadership, he had real power and influence on this team. While he was hosting a party after hours, he was also breaking the law by providing minors with alcohol and cigarettes. And when the parents of these minors found out that he was doing this, who do you think they called? My dad.

My dad handled the situation, professionally and directly. It was a teachable moment as the kitchen manager didn't understand how his time off affected the business. In all fairness, most employees don't. As the owners of the Avenue, my parents held themselves accountable to a different set of rules and responsibilities. My mom and dad set the standard for what was acceptable and what was not. To be clear, this was not about alcohol being served or the employees gathering after work. And for the record, in no way implying that Marci or I didn't hang out with friends or drink before we were legally able to.

My parents set a very high bar for my sister and me, as well as our employees. They provided us with an opportunity to work in a safe and friendly environment and the ability to grow as individuals. I appreciated their willingness to train the team, not just on job-specific duties like peeling boiled potatoes properly or rolling silverware just right. They invested in their employees. As business owners, they took this responsibility to heart. Working at the Avenue was more than just a job. We were all part of something greater than our individual contributions.

Living in a small town felt like someone was always watching or waiting for your next move. These days, no matter where you live—whether in a small town or a major city, with digital technology everywhere, we are all essentially living in a small town. Our lives are accessible via Facebook, Instagram, LinkedIn, Snapchat, etc., blending our personal and professional personas. Plus, there are security video cameras in place everywhere as well.

As I built my career, I did my best to follow in my parents' footsteps. I was mindful of my responsibilities yet also remained accountable to the business.

⌒

"What in the hell was your team thinking last night?" yelled my boss at me.

"What are you talking about? We all went back to our hotel rooms after dinner to prepare for the day," I said. It was 7am, the morning of one of our biggest venture events.

"Last night, one of your employees was drinking with our sponsors. And she charged over $500 to the sponsor's credit card. She even signed his name. I got an angry phone call this morning," he barked. "Clearly your team didn't listen to you. It's your problem now, so go fix it."

I nodded and walked away. What on earth were they thinking? I have a policy that was strongly communicated and reiterated before any event that we hosted. The policy states that we do not at any time engage with our clients or sponsors in a way that could be misperceived. More specifically, we are allowed to socialize but not drink with these individuals before, during, or after an event. This is a perfect example of why this has always been my policy. Now, just hours before we were to host over 400 people, I had to deal with a team that decided to turn a business event into a personal happy hour.

As the team made its way up the escalator to the open ballroom, I could see on their faces that they were overserved the night before and completely unprepared to work for the next 12 hours. I relayed the conversation I had just had with my boss and explained that there would be consequences for their actions to be dealt with after the event. Two of them rolled their eyes and shuffled off. What they thought was harmless fun and not a big deal turned out to be a very big deal when they learned the credit card that was charged belonged to a partner at a major law firm. And because I was effectively at the top of the reporting structure, I was accountable to our sponsor and responsible for resolving this situation quickly.

I immediately called the sponsor directly after I met with the team. I apologized profusely and told him to send us the invoice for the charges right away for reimbursement. I thanked him for his continued support of our organization and promised that this situation would never happen again under my leadership. I will never forget his response.

"I certainly believe you. I was telling your boss this morning how professional and classy you were to stop by and say hello, but not stay for the party. We got a little out of hand. I appreciate that you were focused on making sure the event was successful." I thanked him for his understanding.

As I dealt with the aftermath of this situation, I was even more convinced my parents knew exactly what they were doing. Having a glass of wine with clients or colleagues is one thing but engaging in behavior that can potentially cause irreparable harm to the company is another. In the end, it cost a team member her job in this situation. I had to hold her accountable. And the other team members learned where the bar was set.

My past experiences shaped the expectation I set for myself and for others in my organization. Accountability doesn't stop just because you've left the office for the day. Taking responsibility for your work matters. And if we all do our best to do right by our clients—to do what is right in business—it will only add to the success and longevity of your business.

⌁

"Unfortunately, Julie, you just didn't execute," she said with a sigh.

Fully aware that my client was trying to use my own words against me, I took a deep breath and tried to quell my anger.

As soon as she said it, the CEO of the client company immediately started to apologize. He said that in no way was this the intent of this call. They merely had made the decision to not renew their existing contract, due to funding and product delays. He was sorry that the conversation had gone so far off script.

But all that being said, I felt compelled to set the record straight.

"I am completely offended that you would even make this statement. My team had executed against all of the project goals and objectives for the last year. Our results improved each month, as shown in the analytics reports that we provided. If you do not wish to renew the contact, that is completely fine. But don't blame my team for those items that fall outside of our responsibility." I committed to transferring all final files or working files to the client and ended the conference call.

As I recounted this story to Susan, I became even more enraged. We effectively launched multiple brands for this client, from logo to packaging to e-commerce to digital marketing. The client praised our work. I even extended my time, providing business consulting as the client looked at potential investors and partners, at no additional cost. We executed seamlessly against the scope of work that we were responsible for. We remained committed to doing the work and for driving results.

Well, so what happened? My firm had been originally hired to develop a brand, to help our client reach potential customers, and then to drive revenue. However, the client wasn't able to complete the manufacturing of its products due to missing components. Their lack of success had to do with their poor production process; it had nothing to do with us. I refer to this as the client's failure to launch. Unfortunately, our client wanted to hold my team accountable for this failure, despite this obligation being outside of our contracted responsibilities. Sadly, in my industry, this happens quite frequently.

In my career, I've consulted with thousands of companies on business, go-to market, and marketing strategy. Our firm has built a solid portfolio of success stories. Sometimes, we end up stepping in to manage or execute areas of the business that we were not hired to assist with. Our clients expect us to perform this work even if those responsibilities fall well outside of the agreed-upon contract. In short, we are being held accountable for work that does not contractually fall within our areas of responsibility.

It's tricky to navigate this situation well. We've had many clients who are more than happy to partner with our team in lock-step, but we've had others, much like in the above story, who want to hold us accountable for their failures.

I started Junction because I wanted to bridge the gap between real business strategy and the execution of strategy—the tactical road map designed to reach success. I believe in our team and in our ability to execute the responsibilities we are tasked with. I take my role in our clients' businesses very seriously. I am careful not to overpromise and then underdeliver. And I will often share with potential clients that we are not the agency who is going to tell them what they want to hear; rather, we are going to tell them what they need to hear so as to make our engagement as effective as possible. Otherwise, it's all too easy to blame Junction when the result isn't success.

It's taken me many years to manage what comes with being accountable for Junction, its employees, and its clients. Some days, I feel like I have a ton of bricks in my briefcase. Many days, I am thankful for my incredible team for taking responsibility and accountability for their role at Junction and with our clients.

I joke that sometimes that I feel like I need to lower the bar, to set the expectation where I know all others will reach. As I am sure you can imagine, I would never actually consider this as an option. After all, I am my parents' daughter. They have taught me well.

My dad always says to my sister and me, "Girls, as the leader of your own company, you will always have a target on your back. You can't avoid it. You must accept that the hits will keep coming as long as you are out in front. If you don't like it, don't be out in front."

Dad's words may be considered harsh, but they are the hard truth. If you aren't prepared to take on the responsibility and accountability of owning a business, the entrepreneurial journey might not be the best choice for you.

However, if you are prepared, just adjust the target, and keep on moving forward.

IMPORTANT DETAILS

» As an entrepreneur, you will find that at the end of the day, responsibility and accountability for the business will fall on you.

» Be accountable and take responsibility for all actions, whether your own or by others in your organization.

» As the leader, you will have a target on your back. Don't get out in front if you aren't prepared to take the hits.

CHAPTER ELEVEN

⌒

THE GENERATIONAL DIVIDE

While COVID-19 usually gets the blame for the office shake-up and the fight against the return to work, the truth is, the issues with the new adaptive workforce were in play long before COVID-19 began, indicative of an environment now accommodating multiple workforce generations.

We now have baby boomers (born 1946–1964), Generation X (born 1965–1980), millennials (born 1981–1996), and Generation Z (born 1997 and after) all fighting for a seat at the table. It's dynamic, to say the least, with a lot of noise around adapting to meet the rising demands of the latest generation to enter the workforce. Researchers, polls, and surveys lean toward creating the kind of environment that is expected by the workforce yet offer no solution to bridging this generational divide.

More so in the last five years, it's become more apparent how far apart we are in so many areas. While I hope that I've done a good job navigating the changes, I've definitely learned more about how to build a multigenerational team. Unfortunately, as business owners, we find ourselves in unchartered territory with no "one size fits all" approach to accommodating four generations in the office.

As we look to narrow the generational divide, while I could write an entire book on the subject, I will share the personal experiences that are helping shape my own perspective. Tales for the ages, pun intended!

YOU SAID, WHAT?

"Oh my gosh, Julie," one of my younger employees in her early 20s said as she walked into my office. "I am so tired this morning. I met this guy at a bar last night. We ended up back at my place and were up until almost 5am. I hope he calls me today. It's not like me to have a one-night stand..." The words continued to roll out of her mouth. I looked up from my computer station and nodded as if I were actively listening.

Rarely, if ever, am I speechless. I muttered something to the effect of "Oh, forgive me, but Susan just Skyped me and she needs to talk to me immediately about a client. Okay?"

"Of course, the last thing you need is to hear about my dating life." She smiled as she walked out of my office.

So many emotions and thoughts ran through my mind at one time. Should I know this information? How do I respond? Could I be held liable for not engaging with her? Do I look like her bestie? What kind of person or employee shares this kind of private information with the CEO of the company, as freely as though we are discussing our favorite drink from Starbucks? Is this disrespectful? Does this violate any HR policies? Generation Z or not, this is not appropriate watercooler conversation.

Generation Z are known as the digital natives, the generation who grew up with access to information at their fingertips and with social platforms like Snapchat and Instagram, among others. No personal conversation is seemingly off-limits and not a detail is spared. Where along the way did we lose the common respect for boundaries in communications, not just with management but also employees? After I was subjected to her dating story, I overheard her sharing it with other employees, which caused a bit of discomfort among the team. It seemed no one in the office was particularly interested in her sex-capades story, for which I was relieved. As the employer though, I needed to address what was considered acceptable in our workplace and what was not acceptable from a policy perspective.

Looking back, in my early 20s, I was in a long-term relationship with someone who was friendly with my boss and his wife. The four of us were all part of a similar social circle surrounding our work endeavors. My boyfriend and I both made the decision to keep our relationship completely private, ensuring that our personal lives didn't blend with our professional lives. As a young female in business, I was friendly enough with my co-workers to exchange weekend plans or stories, but under no circumstance would I share information about who I was or was not dating.

I vividly remember when my relationship ended, my boss told me about my former boyfriend's dating life and travel plans for the following weekend. To avoid blowing my cover, which I had kept intact for nearly two years, I walked to the ladies' restroom, hid in a stall, and cried. I pulled myself together and walked back to my office, no one the wiser. Outside of a few photos from work events, there wasn't a digital trace that our relationship even existed. To this day, I wonder if either my boss or his wife ever knew.

We spend more time at work with our co-workers than with our friends and family. Getting to know each other is part of that social experience. While I hope to foster an environment where we can share personal celebrations like the birth of a child or sympathize in the event of a death, I have learned that setting boundaries between our personal and professional lives is just good business.

It's also important to note that if an employee is willing to not just cross the boundary but to jump clearly over the line, it says a lot about what impact this individual could have on your team, your clients, and the overall perception of your business. When you do find yourself speechless, find your way out of the conversation. No response is often the best response.

Here's another example of what I mean from a conversation I had not long ago:

"My friends are planning on renting an Airbnb and traveling around the world since their work offices are still on remote," an employee said to me when discussing the impact of COVID on business. "They can work whenever they want and travel to the places they want to visit. It's a win-win."

"For whom?" I asked. "It doesn't seem like a sustainable way to grow a business based on my experience. I imagine it would be difficult to travel around the world and to remain disciplined enough to make work a real focus."

"So, you say," the female employee retorted somewhat indignantly.

This was just another example of a casual conversation around the office. Another conversation about the evolving work environment. I always find it curious when employees approach me with a perspective about how the grass is greener for their friends at other workplaces. Another reminder of how our work environment doesn't measure up to living on a catamaran in the US Virgin Islands. For me, these conversations are not productive. I get presented with a litany of reasons why employers should let employees do what they want, as opposed to what employees can do to support the organization they work for. The wants, needs, and motivations of the employee come first, the bottom line of the business second?!

During the COVID shutdown, our offices closed for in-person attendance for the first six weeks. After that, our team returned to the office as we all had socially distanced offices and only half of the team works from the headquarters. We have continued to adapt our policy as we go. I've learned from experience that full remote is not the best way to promote a collaborative culture while also keeping employees driven to perform—and perform well.

I remember when Marissa Mayer, the former CEO of Yahoo!, mandated that all her employees get back to the office, and thus moving away from a hybrid model. She received a lot of negative feedback on her efforts, but in my opinion, she was right to do so. When my team was dealing with the Yahoo! team, often-times, we'd be waiting for a team member to get breakfast from the food truck outside or talking over the sounds of Disneyland roller coasters in the background. You read that right: folks who were charged to manage millions of dollars in advertising were at Disneyland with their kids. While I am sure this was not all employees, at the time, I didn't feel this was an acceptable work culture.

From what I can see, not every employee is a great employee when working from home. It requires great discipline and focus to not be distracted by the laundry, dishes in the sink, or the possibility of a midday nap. What I can offer is this—create a work environment that you can manage, effectively. Don't just offer hybrid or remote because researchers tell you that is the expectation. Make the best decisions to promote productivity and results for *your* business. Add incentives for those employees to earn a hybrid schedule as performance dictates it.

I admit, it's been a struggle to adapt my own perspectives on hybrid work environments. As a young professional, I would never dare to demand to work from home or even ask for accommodations to fit my lifestyle. Even as a CEO, I hold myself accountable to being present, in person, at the office even though there are days I'd love to lounge comfortably at home. I am listening though to the feedback that I receive from employees and making changes that I feel I can consistently support.

AND THE WINNER IS?!

"Did you finish Donna's list?" the manager asked the dishwasher.

"I did one or two things on the list," replied the dishwasher.

"You better get to work if you want to get out of work on time today," said the manager.

At the Avenue, Donna (more affectionately called Mom) was known for her detailed task lists, which were presented to the staff, whether a waitress or a dishwasher, at the beginning of each shift. She was often met with resistance as these lists were as comprehensive as possible. And if the tasks on the list were not completed by the end of the shift, she would remind you that you were required to finish all of the tasks before leaving for the day. If you tried to leave without completing them, she would remind you of the consequences. It's important to note, by the way, that the lists included tasks that could feasibly be accomplished in a shift.

Much of the pushback on these tasks came from our millennials, mostly teenagers at the time. They would complain openly to the kitchen managers and often to my sister Marci or me. We'd hear excuses about a baseball practice that was hard that day or being late to hang with friends. We would even have parents call in to ask for leniency because their son or daughter was tired from sports practice or a game. Those parent phone calls were the basis of many conversations among my family. At the time, I remember thinking how odd it was that a parent was telling an employer to "ease up" on their 17-year-old because he was tired.

As a parent, I really can't imagine ever calling my daughter's future employer to ask for leniency. As an employer, I can only imagine how I would respond if I received a phone call like that.

In the end, Donna's List would remain part of the daily routine at the restaurant, even long after my parents sold it. Those lists applied to all employees whether you were 17 or 45. My mom was tough. She was fair. If you wanted to work at the Avenue, my mom was not afraid to tell you what was expected. One's age or generation wasn't even a consideration for her. I respect that about her.

Born in the late 70s and a product of the 80s, Generation X is known for being resourceful. We remember a time before technology. We were expected to get up off the couch to change the TV channel. We spent our days outside. Many of us were latchkey kids, fiercely independent. We loved disposable cameras to capture moments and memories on a single role of film, safe from being published online. We found answers to questions in encyclopedias and card catalogues. And if we didn't know how to do something, we were forced to figure it out on our own. We were raised by baby boomers and didn't dare challenge that generation, who remain to this day an essential part of the fabric of the American dream.

⌒

"This family?!" I texted to my cousins, all part of a perpetual group chat. It was in response to discussion around one of our businesses being on the cutting edge of something really important in the medical field. Never surprised by the ingenuity and entrepreneurial spirit that many of us possess. At our family reunions, as more than 40 of us gather to celebrate each year, I am proud to look around the room and find myself in the company of overachievers in our respective fields. We often joke at how our Cropp blood runs through us and fuels us.

My grandparents and their siblings made choices to advance in their careers, not out of entitlement but survival. As small business owners in the 50s, they were considered the disruptors by charting their own course as entrepreneurs. They didn't come from great wealth or advantaged circumstances. But they knew how to work hard and make do with what they had. I have a great deal of admiration for the challenges they faced, knowing that the world was evolving into a world built for entrepreneurs. My aunts, uncles, and parents followed in those footsteps, building new businesses. And because of this, I was able to chart my own path forward as a small business owner and entrepreneur. My work ethic is reflective of those that came before me. As you've learned from the previous chapters, I didn't wait for praise or a pat on the back. I kept my head down and just focused on earning my seat at the table based on the merits of my work.

I was more than fortunate to have learned that you can get what you want—if you work hard to get it. No handouts, no freebies, no get rich quick. Work is hard. Life is hard. You will be a winner. You will also fail from time to time. Accept the reality that we don't all receive participation trophies.

OFFICE SNACKS & PERKS

In today's work environment, it has become happenstance to receive critical feedback from my clients, employees, or partners. Ten years ago, it would be shocking for an employee to tell me directly to my face that this isn't the dream job they had hoped for, that their friends are allowed to play Ping-Pong at other jobs, and that other companies sponsor happy hours every Friday. It's been an adjustment to give these employees the freedom to speak their every thought and wish. While I have a thick skin, some days, I wish I had a suit of armor on to deflect each dagger as they are thrown.

When we look to hire a new team member, I am transparent as to the culture and environment. I actually say, "We don't have a Ping-Pong table or happy hours each Friday." There is a method to my approach with this statement. If candidates seem surprised or taken aback by this or ask what office perks we have, I am able to determine the likelihood of their success at our firm. It's not that I don't think it's fun to play Ping-Pong or have a company happy hour; I don't feel like that should be the reason why a candidate chose to work for an organization. I know, as a Generation Xer, this is no surprise. If I was a millennial or a Zoomer, I might be more apt to hire a Director of Happiness to the chagrin of boomers everywhere. What I do offer is the opportunity to grow one's compensation, earn bonuses, receive generous paid time off, and an abundance of office snacks, including Coca-Cola, ordered based on an employee's preference.

All this to say—happy hours and Ping-Pong work for many companies who are solely focused on attracting younger generations. In most environments, there is more than one generation to make accommodations for. And don't forget that perks don't always correlate with performance.

KEEPING UP WITH TECHNOLOGY

"I am so stressed," I said to Susan. "I haven't taken an exam like this since graduate school, and of all things, it has to be on cybersecurity."

Susan shared the same concern. One of our clients requires our team to be certified on their internal security protocols. We were to take the online course, study, and then pass the exam. The scoring on the exam was difficult and only left room for one or two wrong answers. The results were sent directly back to our clients. We took the online course, copiously took notes, and posted it for team members to study from. We were met with muffled laughter from the millennials in the office.

"Why are you so worried?" one young woman said to us. "When you take the online course, just take a screenshot of the slide on your phone. Then keep your phone handy when taking the test, so you can get the answers from the screenshots." She smiled confidently, and added: "This is how we got through college."

To say I was stunned by her response is putting it mildly. It was a stark generational difference that truly ran a risk of totally ruining the business and our clients. To her, this was common practice in her education and now in her workplace. Just leverage the technology to provide a shortcut, a cheat sheet to ace an exam. Ingenious on one hand, troubling on the other. Our clients expected us to not just take this exam but to fully understand the policies and procedures that we need to follow to comply with security measures in place to protect their organization. If we breached protocol, my firm would ultimately be held responsible. Knowing that an employee took a shortcut—and didn't really learn the information—was also my responsibility to correct. I encouraged the team to study the information and shared with them the liability concerns that I had. I still studied the old-fashioned way and passed with flying colors.

For baby boomers and Generation X, this story invokes frustration, as we adapt to the work habits of the younger generations. Millennials and Zoomers grew up with technology in its current form, whereas boomers and Generation X have spent the last 30 years learning new technology or a new version of the same technology. What do I mean by this?

Google launched in 1998. I remember visiting one of the computer labs in the college library to use Google for the first time. "Google" wasn't considered a verb yet. It was simply a box on a computer screen to fill in. Most of what I searched for resulted in less than ten results. Since then, look at how powerful Google has become. With each iteration or launch of a new Google product, I am exhausted just thinking about learning another new function or feature. I am in my 40s; imagine how this feels for the baby boomers in the office? A generation that saw the first color television and the very first personal computer in 1976. And a generation that learned how to use the only resources they had to get the work done. There were no shortcuts or a Wikipedia of answers to reference. As technology evolved, these two generations adapted, learned, relearned, etc., and continue to learn as systems are upgraded.

At the Avenue, I remember the year my parents installed a new point-of-sale system, the first in the restaurant in nearly 40 years. From a business perspective, it was the best solution to automate and improve our processes in managing the front of the restaurant and the kitchen. During the training, we had numerous employees, who had been with the restaurant for decades, fight the process of learning the new system. Then, after using the system on a busy Sunday during the lunch rush, attitudes shifted, and complaints lessened as the new system really saved a lot of time and steps. The key to its success was patience. Not every employee learned at the same pace or understood all of the features at the same time. Over time, we all adapted to the new system as if we'd never operated this way without it.

As the CEO, I've been accused of being old-school in the workplace. My processes and work habits have been referred to as archaic. "There is a faster way." "That takes too long." "Don't you know you can speak directly into the computer instead of typing." Yes, I am fully aware of these things. But for me, those outdated processes are what keep me on time and task. What most don't understand is that my process enables me to be really effective and thorough at my job. In the process of writing and then typing the notes, I am committing those notes to memory. I am paying close attention to the details, which are required to be successful as the owner of this company. Much like that security exam, just because there is an easier way doesn't mean that it's a better way, especially in the workplace.

We all bring work habits, technical proficiency, and legacy knowledge to the team. There needs to be a greater appreciation for each other's differences. I guarantee you that if the internet suddenly went away, we'd need all of our collective skill sets to figure out how to move business forward.

MY ADVICE?

From generation to generation, the fundamentals of building a business have remained the same. While technology, work environments, and general attitudes have evolved far beyond what my grandparents could have imagined, the generational divide is not as far apart as we think. We must be mindful of each other, our expertise, and what our previous experience brings to the current day. We must listen and learn. While we may have a different approach, we cannot lose sight that we are all working toward a common goal.

We should all be proud of our generational titles. I would be remiss if I didn't also note that I've come to admire baby boomers, millennials, and Zoomers. Baby boomers represent one of our greatest generations. I attribute a lot of my success to being able to learn from great business owners, who started a business, with the cards stacked against them. I admire millennials for not being afraid to ask for what they want and for what they feel they deserve. I could have benefited from that knowledge early in my career. And Generation Z is a welcome breath of fresh air, a generation that isn't afraid to ask for what they want but willing to work hard to prove their value.

I've spent a lot of time over the years thinking about happy hours, flex days, hybrid schedules, office perks, etc. While I will acquiesce on a few items, I will not change who I am or what type of business I want to create. That isn't what got me here. And it won't get me to where I want to go.

As an entrepreneur, it is within your power to determine what type of business you want to have. While you will need to be mindful of a multigenerational workplace, you will have the opportunity to create a business environment that you are proud of. Not all people will be on board with your approach, policies, or culture. And that is okay. Do your best to listen to all of the voices in the room, not just the generation that speaks the loudest.

Eventually I realized that my business and employees achieve great things and deliver exceptional results, not because of the snacks or a hybrid work schedule, but because we all show up to work every day—and we work hard. We are accepting of each other's experiences and appreciate the expertise that we each contribute, and our environment is reflective of that—not our age.

IMPORTANT DETAILS

> » Build a workplace culture that empowers all generations and just doesn't cater to the loudest group.
> » We all bring knowledge, experience, and perspective to the workplace. Listen and learn from each other.
> » Create a business environment that you are truly proud of.

CHAPTER TWELVE

⌒

PLANNING FOR THE EXIT

One of the great ironies of starting your own business and then running it is that too few entrepreneurs ever take the time to give their exit strategy any real thought or serious consideration. This chapter is meant to have you at least recognize that there will come a time when you need to plan out your exit from the firm. Of course, every start-up business is unique and different; so is every entrepreneur. But as you progress and build your company into a real success, you will need to someday have to figure out what the next step will be for you. I've written this chapter to provide some general thoughts and insights for you.

⌒

Several years ago, my father sat down with my sister Marci and me for an important conversation.

"Do either of you want to be the next owner at the Avenue?" he asked.

With a fear of disappointing my family, I quietly replied, "No." Marci, who had already launched her career as a mechanical engineer, had the same response. Our reasons and motivations were different, but the answer was still the same.

Of course, it would have been the perfect succession plan. My parents would transition ownership of their restaurant over time to my sister or me, with us eventually becoming full owners of the Avenue. Unfortunately, succession wasn't really an option in this case. Marci and I were too young to commit to the Avenue being our future, as we had yet to explore our own career paths. We also knew that working at the Avenue was a sunup-to-sundown kind of commitment. Plus at the time, we only carried a fraction of the responsibilities that my parents had as the business owners.

Prior to my parents buying the restaurant, there had been two other owners. Both owners stayed at the helm for nearly 20 years each before selling. It was a grueling business. Statistically, most restaurants don't even survive five years let alone reach success 10 years in the business. My parents didn't have a compass or a road map to follow. But they did listen to the previous owners of the restaurant, who spoke from experience. One even noted that they should have sold eight years before they did. Burnout was a real thing in this business. My dad and mom set their intention on being in the restaurant business for 10 years, but no more.

For my parents, the goal was to grow the revenue year over year, such that in 10 years, the restaurant would be more valuable and attractive to a potential buyer. As they neared that 10-year mark, my parents had to look at what options they had for exiting the business. As it turned out, one of our employees who had worked at the restaurant since he was 14 years old was seriously interested in becoming the next owner. My dad will tell you that this was the best exit strategy, one that allowed him to cash out his investment yet sell to someone who had become like family in the 10 years we'd worked with him. The deal ultimately went through as planned with a longtime employee becoming the new owner of the restaurant.

Selling the Avenue was a bittersweet moment for all of us, including the employees and our customers. That being said, it was exciting and fulfilling to watch my parents reap their rewards after sacrificing so much, putting in those long days and often sleepless nights. They had grown the business, far exceeding any revenue goal or expectation they had originally set. But more importantly, they offered employees an opportunity to be part of the Avenue family, which was so much more than just a job. Our customers also became like an extension of our team, stopping in every time they passed through town or visited each day for a meal and a casual conversation. There was a great amount of pride and respect for the new owner, who had started at the Avenue as a dishwasher. The transition didn't feel as hard knowing that one of our own was going to be taking over the business, following in the footsteps of each owner at the Avenue. While the new owner would go on to make changes to the menu and décor, the core team remained the same, as did our customers.

Overall, this proved to be a great example of how to successfully exit a business. This was a classic case of how hard work can lead to even greater rewards. But be forewarned, this will not be the case for all business owners. The truth is, as noted, too many entrepreneurs fail to plan for an exit strategy, leaving them without an opportunity to either maximize the financial value of the business or to see it thrive and then grow under the watch of a new owner.

I encourage anyone who is building or growing a business to think about where you would like your enterprise to go. Think about what you want to take from this business. Not just today, but in the future. It might feel strange to plan for an exit when you are just beginning a business. However, it keeps you always looking forward to what is next. Some of you might decide to build a business, earn as much as you can, and then sell it or just close it when you are ready to retire. Many of you will spend years chasing the golden ticket, the promise of a big financial gain.

Whatever you decide, be sure to develop your exit plan well in advance, detail the steps that will take you where you want to go. And most importantly, have the courage to modify that plan as you go, adjusting for success or failure along the way.

As you develop your approach, be sure to consider all of the options for successfully selling your business. What are the best options for planning your exit? If you haven't started to explore the exit strategy, let me share a few potential options to consider:

SUCCESSION PLANNING

Family succession or a legacy exit refers to the idea of keeping the business in the family, passing on the company to a family member. This can prove beneficial as the family member likely has significant knowledge or experience working the business and is better prepared to take over the day-to-day responsibilities of the business. And in most cases, as the owner, you can stay involved as an advisor or consultant to assist with the transition.

It's important to note, with family succession, it takes a great deal of patience as often the lines between personal and professional get blurred. Finances and emotions can sometimes get in the way of a successful handoff.

As an example, if my parents were to sell the Avenue to my sister and me, they would have expected that we pay them the purchase price. Succession doesn't mean that you are given the business to run; you will still need financial investment in order to successfully transfer the business. Remember that in any business exchange, there is a financial investment from one party and a financial gain for the original business owner. I've seen deals stall when family members get in heated arguments over business valuation and money. When dealing with family members, it might be best to hire an external business advisor to keep the conversations calm and the negotiations fair.

MERGERS & ACQUISITIONS

This strategy is very popular for start-ups and entrepreneurs. In this case, you would sell your business to another company, which is looking to either increase their market share, eliminate competing brands, or to acquire specialized talent or products. In this kind of situation, you would have more of a chance of controlling the price negotiations and setting the terms of the sale. You can sell your business for a multiple of revenues, which leans in favor of the entrepreneurs.

What does this mean? As you build your business, I recommend that you keep at least three years of financial projections so that you can measure last year, the current year, and what you project for the following year. You can find financial projections templates online to use as a guide or reference point. Within the financial documentation, you will outline revenue and expenses. As you engage in the M&A process, it is critical to have a strong financial understanding of what your business is actually worth. Valuation can be determined in multiple ways. If you are a service-based business, M&A investors will look for companies that have a majority of contracts with recurring revenue and a healthy and consistent profit margin over the last three fiscal years. If you are a product-based company, investors will look at any intellectual property that you might have, revenue, and profit margin as well. All investors are looking for opportunities that are going to deliver product, people, and profit. Remember that investors will have different criteria or ways to evaluate the business. Be sure to research and read as many articles as possible or books to educate yourself on what to expect.

Despite the popularity of M&A opportunities, it's vitally important to have experts assist with the successful sale of the business. If you haven't gone through this process before, business owners tend to either leave money on the table or get greedy and risk losing the entire deal. Don't go into the deal unprepared.

"Well, Julie, after I pay our attorneys and our M&A team, this is really what the value of your business is," an investor once told me after reviewing the financials. An investor reached out to me to see if I was interested in selling my business. He presented me with a ridiculously insulting number, grossly undervaluing the growth trends and overall business value.

I didn't flinch.

"Interesting. Based on my growth over the last three years and the projections for the trailing 24 months, I stand to make double that number just in profit next year. And I honestly don't have to sell," I responded directly.

He pushed back.

"To be fair though, Julie, you have to decide who would really want your business. Do you want to sell this to an equity investor or sell to a larger agency? Are you prepared to become a mid-level manager at a new firm working for a $100,000 salary?"

As he spoke, I could feel my blood start to boil. I knew this tactic all too well, as I had a view from his side of the table earlier in my career. Unfortunately for him, I wasn't taking the bait. I had pulled together my financials and thoroughly reviewed the information leading up to this meeting. I had already projected what a valuation could potentially provide based on my revenue, forecasted revenue, and profit margins. His tactic was to present the lowest possible offer to see if that would be enticing. Clearly, it didn't align with my expectations.

I left the meeting feeling frustrated. I wasn't even the one who asked for the meeting. And yet, I left feeling anger, disappointment, and uncertainty. His offer was insulting. I was excited coming into this meeting, for a seat at the table. And I felt grateful for this opportunity to be presented with an offer, even if it wasn't the best deal for me at the time.

SELLING TO A PARTNER OR INVESTOR

Some business owners look to sell their share of the business to a partner or a venture capital investor. By selling to a partner in the business, that reduces the potential for business disruption, keeping the business stable during the transition. Since this person also has a vested interest in the business, the terms of the deal are often fair and set the new owner up for success.

When dealing with a venture capital investor, it's critical to understand the terms of the sale and how this sale will affect the overall success of the business and what your role is expected to be going forward, post the transaction.

Do your research. Understand what the process is from beginning to end. There are also other options to consider outside of those that I already have presented. And if you don't have experience in this area, I strongly encourage you to identify the right partners, experts who can assist in managing the technical details of the transaction. Leverage your professional connections to identify potential partners rather than just doing a simple search online. You want to have a clear understanding of who the advisors are and what it was like to work with them. A referral from a colleague is always a great way to start. Be sure to evaluate a minimum of three different candidates for each advisory role. Who should be on your team of advisors? Select a legal advisor who has experience working with entrepreneurs and business. If you are a technology company, make sure they have experience working with technology companies. Hire a financial advisor who has successfully managed sale of business transactions. For example, every business should have a CPA to manage the financials; however, most CPAs aren't well versed in the kind of financial expertise required to prepare a company for sale. Develop a trusted relationship with these partners as they will be handling your most valuable assets and your money. And as I've mentioned before, trust but verify.

In my case, I've been very lucky. With my experience in first working for an entrepreneurship institute, a venture capital organization, my parents' restaurant, and being married to a serial entrepreneur, I've become a sponge, soaking in any and every detail that I can that is related to building, growing, and selling a business. I've been fortunate to see former clients, colleagues, or family members sell businesses. My husband has sold many businesses in the time that we've been together. As a result, I have intimate knowledge of what financial documentation is required, how negotiations work, and the importance of maximizing the value of the deal. It's important to note that I've seen incredible exits, but I've also witnessed deals end badly. I had a front-row seat, watching the process from the initial conversation to the final signature.

Be sure to surround yourself with like-minded people who may be on a similar journey or who work with entrepreneurs. Casual conversation can often turn into a kind of impromptu master class, providing you with context and real insights on how to best maneuver the end stages of owning your business. Listen to both the good and the bad.

Process is an integral part of the exit but it's not the only thing to be focused on. From what I can see, building a sound and thorough exit strategy takes time, and when doing it, you always need to be aware of your employees.

⌣

"Did you hear the news?" he whispered as he walked into my office.

"No, what did I miss?" I answered.

"There are a few suits here looking and poking around. I think the CEO is selling the business," he said.

By lunchtime, the word had spread quickly throughout the office that this could be the new owners checking things out. With little communication from leadership, our imaginations started to get the best of us. We went from exhilaration of possible promotions and big raises to the cold reality that a majority of the company would be fired.

The longer we went without information, the more dejected we became. Eventually, weeks later, our leadership team did in fact tell us that they were in serious discussions with another firm, but the negotiations had stalled. As an employee, I understood that it was not my business to know what the CEO was planning for. However, as a smaller agency, he also knew that there were whispers around the office. A simple communication could have dispelled the fear among the team, as it created strong reactions across the board. We went from being actively engaged in our day-to-day roles to now updating our resumes and looking for opportunities, just in case.

Never forget: people are the lifeblood of any business. These individuals have chosen this business as their place of employment. They come to work every day, focused on executing your vision to reach the goals that you have set for the firm. As the owner, it can be easy to get caught up in the details of the transaction and to lose sight of the people supporting the business. I don't advocate that you share the details of exploratory conversations or initial discussions around the sale of the business. As you get closer to signing letters of intent or contracts, though, that's the time to communicate, communicate, communicate. It's human nature for employees to be concerned or uncertain about what this means. No communication could cost you a lot of money and unrest before the ink is even dry.

⌒

"Want to try the new restaurant at the Avenue?" I asked my dad on a recent trip to Gettysburg.

"Sure, I have not been in there since it became a noodle restaurant," he said.

It had been more than 15 years since I'd eaten at the Avenue. Since we sold the restaurant, ownership had changed hands a few times. As of 2020, it was still a casual dining restaurant serving breakfast, lunch, and dinner. Now it's a noodle house with sushi. As we walked into the restaurant, I was surprised at how the experience struck me. I was overcome by a flurry of emotion. As we were ushered to a booth, I took the seat that faced the street.

Almost as if by habit, my dad and I scanned the dining rooms, looking for what was different. The barstools were still there, minus one or two that had been removed. The booths' vinyl coverings had been updated, in a more ornate pattern, one that neither of us cared for. The tile floors were exactly as we'd left them, although we both joked that the grout could use a good cleaning. We both laughed recalling my teenage trauma of scrubbing those with a toothbrush.

"Yes, but those floors looked great, didn't they?" my dad said, smiling.

"The bones are still here. Look at the old Avenue sign in the back dining room. It's the original logo. I can't believe it's still here," I said as I got up out of my seat to walk toward the old sign.

The bones were in fact still there. The memories still present. And the emotions were very real. We slipped into an hour-long conversation about the grueling days, the long hours, and how great it felt to be able to come back as customers to a place that forever changed our lives. We talked about what could have been, what we should have changed, and if selling it was really the right decision. I still have goose bumps just thinking about the experience.

What you don't often find in business books or podcasts is advice on how to manage the emotions that come with selling a business. It's often the human emotions that make or break the best deals. And when it comes down to putting an actual value on a business, it becomes even more personal.

With my own start-up agency, I've spent over a decade chasing one goal after another after another. I am still reaching, still fighting for every client and every dollar. It's exhilarating to succeed. It pushes me to work harder to reach the next goal. I am proud of our body of work, my team, and how far we've come. But I must be honest, it's also exhausting. There are days when I am paralyzed by the sheer volume of decisions I need to make or by the amount of each payroll the company needs to reach. I am faced with the challenges of hiring in this ever-evolving business environment and adapting our services to meet the demands of our clients. As you well know, the highs are so high, and the lows are so low—an emotional roller coaster.

For me, I try to acknowledge the emotions that come to the surface. I find that the harder I try to ignore them, the more virulent they will become. You don't want to walk away from a negotiation either angry or crying. Listen first, process next, and react later, preferably alone or in the company of your trusted advisors.

⌐⌐

If I were to sell my company, what did I want my role to be? Would I be willing to move back down into middle management?

If I didn't stay on with the company, what would I do? All important questions to answer.

I started my business at the age of 30 and I am only in my 40s now. I spent my waking hours working hard to grow this business, raising my daughters, being a wife, sister, daughter, and friend. And most of those hours are spent at the office. If I suddenly got eight to 10 hours back in my day, how would I spend them? I've got hopefully another 50 years of life left, so that is a lot of time to account for.

Think really hard about this. As entrepreneurs, we are driven to work hard every day, without question. Blood, sweat, and tears are part of our daily method of operating. We are motivated to build, grow, and to look for the next opportunity. It's who we are. It's what we do.

As you can tell, I am passionate about this journey from being a waitress working at my parents' restaurant to successfully running my own business. It's that passion that keeps me looking forward. Always moving toward what's next.

As the adage goes, don't lose sight of the forest for the trees. When you are caught up in growth, hiring employees, and managing the business, it can be difficult to remain focused on what lies ahead.

I started this journey recently married and had no children. I was more fearless and excited about growing a business. As Junction celebrated its 10-year anniversary and my daughters were starting school, I was a little more skeptical and exhausted. As my business continues to grow, reaching new goals, I became more intently focused on what a potential exit could look like. An exit strategy, to me, feels so final in many ways—it represents the end of one dream and the beginning of another. But I embrace it. Catch me on a good day and I will tell you that I am in this for another 20 years. On a bad day, I might say, I can be found on a catamaran in the British Virgin Islands. Every day, I am filled with gratitude that this is my journey as a business owner. The exit is always top of mind as I set my intention for each day. Trust that I have a plan, well, two. This should not surprise you. And I can't wait to see how this turns out.

As you contemplate the exit, recognize and celebrate this incredible next step in the journey. Entrepreneurs and business owners everywhere celebrate with you. It represents your success—it totally validates all of your hard work.

IMPORTANT DETAILS

» Think forward in business. Have an idea of where you would like your business to go.

» Educate yourself on the process of selling your business. Be prepared.

» Celebrate every moment of this journey—not just the exit.

EPILOGUE

When I boarded the plane for Paris, at just 21 years of age, I remember feeling butterflies and fear as I walked into the plane. I had just said my good-byes to my parents, and I knew they were waiting inside the terminal, looking out the large windows at the plane. I'm sure they were feeling those same butterflies, terrified that their little girl was moving to a foreign county. It was then that I made up my mind to always look forward and, in every situation thereafter, whenever I was taking a leap of faith into unknown territory.

Whether a superstition or an old wives' tale, I only challenged this rule on two occasions in my life. The first time was in 2006, after attending a friend's destination wedding in Costa Rica. The wedding party and guests were all huddled around at the airport on the last day, waiting for our flights to take us back to our everyday lives. As I was boarding my plane for Philadelphia, I felt this sudden and irrepressible urge to look behind me, desperate to peer down into the boarding area. I could see Steve, who I had just met at the wedding, typing on his computer. Even though I scolded myself for looking back, I knew it meant something far greater than just a glance over my shoulder. Steve later became my husband and partner in life.

The second time was in early 2022. I felt the weight of running a business, managing a household, raising two children, and maintaining appearances even though I was struggling. I was searching for something, so I sifted through 30 years of journals

I had written, searching for inspiration and motivation, in these pages of my past. It served me well; I ultimately found my voice and the words to write this book.

Writing this book triggered emotions and recalled incredible experiences that shaped who I am today. At various times during this process, it shook me to my core. Yet, I am in awe. And I'm reminded of my 20-something-year-old self, who faced unsurmountable hardships and didn't let them break my spirit or my stride. I was fearless. I believed that if I worked hard enough, I could achieve whatever I set out to accomplish. To her, I would say "thank you" for leading the charge, for laying a solid foundation, and for moving forward one step at a time.

Thanks to her, I found strength, confidence, and became a little less afraid each day. Revisiting my past was a reminder of where I had been and just how far I've come. My late Uncle Larry, a lifelong educator, is known affectionately for his signature phrase "from whence we came." From my being a teenager, waiting tables at my parents' restaurant, to becoming a CEO, entrepreneur, and author, that phrase is never lost on me.

From being a small start-up in the basement of my house to building a multimillion-dollar business, while I may not know what the future will hold, I am exceedingly proud of the efforts and the people who have helped make this little girl's dream into a reality. This book is a reflection of that journey. And I have learned that there is real value in looking back to find your way forward. My advice? When you are building a business, solving problems, and managing a team of people, know that it's hard to pause for a moment to acknowledge one's success. Being an entrepreneur is indeed something to celebrate. It's not the easiest path. If it were easy, everyone would do it. But if you won't take a chance on yourself, who will? I did. I invested my time, my money, and my career to build an organization that embodied what I was so desperate to find. I wanted a safe space to learn, to grow, and to generate positive impact on my colleagues and clients. And that is exactly what I strive to do every day.

Trust your instinct. And don't ever stop moving forward. Be grateful for each stage of this business, whether it brings challenges or triumphs. It is in those moments, the rising and falling, that you evolve. You become a better entrepreneur and what I like to think is the best version of yourself.

Whether you are just starting your career or your first business, I wish you incredible success with just the right amount of failure. Stay humble. Be kind. Be impactful. Earn it.

And when in doubt, just repeat to yourself, *"I'm fine. It's fine. It's going to be fine."* Trust me.

ABOUT THE AUTHOR

Julie is a respected and trusted leader in business communities that extend from the Northeast (Philadelphia, New York City, and D.C.) to the Southeast (including the Greater Atlanta region and Charleston, South Carolina) that include CEOs and entrepreneurs of small to midsize businesses as well as the Fortune 1000. As a CEO of Junction Creative, founded in 2009, she has consulted or completed work for more than 450 brands in the last 15 years, driving millions of dollars in revenue growth for her clients.

It was this experience that inspired Julie to share an authentic story about launching and growing a business. Words have the power to motivate and influence people. The right words have the ability to inspire. Julie knew at a young age that she wanted to write a book, but it took a little over 20 years for her to write this story, an authentic perspective of an entrepreneur starting and growing a business. From her days waitressing for the family business, to starting her career, then pursuing a dream of creating an award-winning digital marketing agency, Julie shares real stories about what it's really like to be an entrepreneur.

To learn more about Junction Creative or
for speaking inquiries, please contact
Julie@Juliecroppgareleck.com!

ACKNOWLEDGEMENTS

For those who know and love me, I've always been a bit of a storyteller. While the stories in this book seem so unbelievable—believe me, they are all true. I had promised myself that—someday—I would write a book about them all. There were many nights over the course of several years when I sat down at my computer to start this book. But the truth was, I was unsure of where to begin and what type of entrepreneurial story I wanted to tell.

Until now.

A journey starts with a single step. Writing this book started with a single word. A simple start- an idea to tell our story of the Avenue Restaurant and the lessons that it so richly taught me as I began and grew my career. And it only seems fitting that this book and these words be an homage to the two people responsible for shaping my work ethic and perspectives from an early age—Mark and Donna Cropp. To Mom and Dad, thank you for being incredible teachers, for listening first, and for loving me always. To my sister and friend, Marci Cropp, your unwavering love and support have given me strength in life. This book is just a small piece of this family's legacy. A permanent reflection of our journey.

To my husband, Steve, thank you for being my partner in life. You respect, encourage, support, and motivate me every day as a mom, a CEO, and now an author. And together we have built an amazing family. To my sweet baby girls, Sophie and Zoe, you've sacrificed many "S-Days" so that Mommy could write. You are my greatest gifts, and I will always love you more.

To my most loyal listeners, my friends and colleagues, thank you for being an incredible sounding board and constant presence in my life. In no particular order, I recognize my lifelong friends. Susan Lynam, the gift of your friendship is one I treasure. We make an incredible team as friends and at work. For that I thank you! Andrea, Kristin, and Kelly, you are such amazing women, professionals, mothers, and great friends. Tiffani Utz, John Utz, Dee Griffith, Rich Griffith, Aaron Cropp, Christine Cropp, Tamara Fridley, Traci Royce, Kiley Royce, Ed and Deb Martin – my cousins by chance, friends by choice – what an incredible life we've traveled together. To Bill Craig, who knew that Naugle Hall at Shippensburg University would be the beginning of a friendship that would last more than 3 decades? A sincere thank you to you and Karie for your continued friendship and partnership along this journey. To my first friend in Atlanta, Jeff Taves, our lunches over the years have served as much-needed therapy sessions, as we navigated life and our careers. For this, I thank you and am grateful for your friendship.

To the team at Junction Creative, thank you for being a part of this organization and for executing against the vision. To those clients who have trusted me over the years, thank you for your confidence in me and my colleagues at Junction Creative.

Acknowledgements

When I made the decision to start the process of writing this book, I knew I needed someone to hold me accountable, to provide critical feedback, and to help me shape the narrative of my story. To Rick Wolff, who passed away just after completing this acknowledgement, I am humbled to have had the opportunity to work with you. While I know you will not be with us to see this book published, this experience of working with one of the greatest in publishing will be remembered as one of the best experiences of my professional career.

To all the many others who have influenced me, I thank you.

Writing this book about how I became a successful entrepreneur has been one of my greatest life experiences, because it forced me to pause and to reflect on how I grew from being a waitress in a small-town restaurant to surviving the travails of the corporate world to eventually becoming the founder and CEO of a thriving start-up.

You know, in a way, my life has come full circle. That's because when I was a little girl, I always aspired to be a writer. At 45 years of age, I dared myself to become one.

NOTES

NOTES

NOTES

NOTES

NOTES